Where Meadows & Gardens Grow

THE EMBROIDERY OF JO BUTCHER

INSPIRATIONS

Introduction

THE ART OF EMBROIDERY is to tell a story with needle and thread. I hope that the designs in this book tell of the love and happiness that embroidery gives to me.

Occasionally in life we get to fulfil a dream; being asked to create this book and inspire others is a dream of mine.

There is joy in the process of creating these pieces of art. From observing nature as I go about daily life, painting the backgrounds and the unexpected paint effects that happen along the way, to choosing the threads and working out which stitches will best represent the impression of the flowers.

My aim is to express the beauty of flowers whilst alluding to a garden or meadow that the observer only realises is stitched on closer inspection. To achieve that look, I don't use hundreds of different stitches; I have a limited selection that I like to use as I know they keep attention on the effect I'm trying to achieve, rather than the stitch itself. And just as I like to mix my paints for the background colours, I also like to mix thread colours in the needle to create subtle colour differences as the flowers are stitched.

These instructions are to inspire you to create your own versions of the projects included. Everyone's embroidery will come out slightly differently, interpreted and expressed through our different perspectives, but trust the development, layer the threads gradually, stand back and observe.

Have fun and enjoy what you create!

- Jo -

Contents

Just a few tips...

THREAD

The ideal length of thread to work with is from fingertip to elbow, although when working the background grass stitches, I recommend using a slightly longer thread than normal.

When stitching a lot of the same colour, thread more than one needle at a time. Divide the strands according to the instructions and thread two or three needles. This saves stopping and starting so often!

To begin a thread, work two or three small split back stitches or use a small knot, as it will not show when there are so many stitches and textures on the picture. Take care not to stitch through the knot when working the embroider

To secure the thread when complete run under the stitches at the back o make small hidden stitches on the reverse.

If it is difficult to pass the needle thread through the fabric, try a larger needle, as this will prev stressing the threads.

I have used stranded cotto could use stranded silk or

RIBBON

When stitching with ri shorter length, appro span or 20cm (8").

Thread the needle that has just bee long tail to secur

ribbon to the needle and prevents it from slipping off.

Use the correct size needle for the ribbon width as this ensures the ribbon is not crushed or damaged by the needle eye.

Where the design is busy, secure the ribbon with a knot. Where there is less detail to hide a knot, leave a small tail at the back and secure with embroidery thread. To finish, leave a tail of ribbon on the back of the work and secure with embroidery thread.

FABRIC

Medium-weight calico (muslin) has been recommended for these projects but any medium weight, even weave cotton would be suitable. If using ribbons, avoid fabrics with a very tight weave as the ribbon will be easily damaged by repeatedly pulling it through the fabric. Once the fabric has been painted and is completely dry, place it into the frame or hoop, ensuring that it is drum tight.

FRAME VERSUS HOOP

All these projects need to be worked held taut on a frame or hoop, due to the long stitches and the tension required. Frames are recommended, but hoops can be used where the entire design will fit inside the hoop.

MOUNT

Having a mount cut to the correct aperture size really does help frame the composition. It focuses the eye on the subject rather than the painted edges.

DETAIL

Remember that when we look at daisies in a meadow or leaves on a tree, we know they are attached by stems and branches but they are not always visible. Therefore, we are not stitching every last detail, but an impression of the subject. Do check that flowers are grounded with a stem where necessary.

KEEP GOING!

Some of my favourite pieces have emerged from the process of rescuing them and this can apply to the painted background or the stitched composition. When you are unsure of your progress, prop your embroidery up with the mount in front and leave it for a while. Come back with fresh eyes and a fresh perspective to see what needs adding!

If there is a small mistake or stitch that is not satisfactory, it is often possible to cover it with a carefully placed flower or stem!

Do not worry if your picture does not look exactly the same as mine; I can never produce two identical pictures, and remember, nature is random and always changing and developing.

Threading a needle with ribbon

This easy method ensures the ribbon is secured firmly to the eye of the needle, ready to begin stitching.

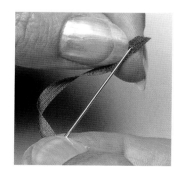

1 / Cut the end of the ribbon diagonally. Thread the ribbon through the needle eye. Slide the needle along the ribbon for approx 5cm (2").

2 / Place the point of the needle approx 5mm (³/₁₆") from the cut end of the ribbon.

3 / Push the needle through the ribbon. Holding the tail in one hand, pull the needle with the other.

4 / The ribbon is now secured and you are ready to begin stitching.

Painting backgrounds

Painting is an art not a science, so the instructions for painting the backgrounds are a guide but not hard rules. Sometimes the painting will go to plan, sometimes it won't, and every now and then you will produce a beautiful background but not know exactly how you did it!

My advice is to play with the paints, experiment, get to know the colours and the results of combining them. If you're starting from scratch, buy a small artists palette by a recognised art company, containing at least two shades of yellow and two shades of blue, ideally a combination of the following.

> *lemon yellow hue /*
> *cadmium yellow pale hue /*
> *cadmium yellow hue /*
> *yellow ochre*

> *cerulean blue /*
> *cobalt blue /*
> *ultramarine blue*

Start with painting small squares of each of your palette colours, then squares of mixed colours, labelling them as you go for future reference. Discover the effects of adding paint to wet paint, damp paint and dry paint. Use a white palette or plate to mix so that you can see the true colours.

All the projects have listed the paint colours to use but you may find that your personal palette differs to mine. The light and the sky can be different shades of

blue depending on where you are and you may want to interpret the colours differently, to add a little ultramarine to your cobalt blue for example.

When painting the sky use the brush in a horizontal direction, for the grass use paint strokes in a vertical direction. Use good quality watercolour sable brushes.

> Size 12 for applying wash
> Size 6 for mixing colours and covering smaller areas
> Size 2 for details and wispy grasses

Drying times will vary depending on your environment, but always dry flat on plain weave cloths as they prevent the paint being transferred to the surfaces below. Do not carry vertically or hang the painted background up to dry as the paint will run off. Also, if the painted fabric is rested on a textured background, the paint will congregate on any details.

When the paint is fully dry, press the fabric, using plain weave pressing cloths to protect your iron and ironing board. By pressing the colours, it prevents them running if further painting is added, for example, when adding the sea.

The fabric needs to be able to hold the paint on top, not seep into the weave as this dilutes the colour. My advice is if you have calico or similar cotton in your fabric stash, have a play with the paints and observe what results you achieve and if you like the effects.

Depending on the calico, the painted area may shrink slightly, and this can usually be remedied by stretching and ironing. It is recommended that you do not pre-shrink and wash the fabric yourself as the creases that form whilst washing are exceedingly difficult to remove.

The dimensions of fabric required for each project are listed with each design. All include a good margin as I prefer to paint a larger area. Then, using a mount cut with the relevant aperture measurements, decide which area of the painted background is preferable. Allowing extra space with your painting means if there is a daub of paint that you do or don't want to include or strategically can't place a stitch over, this gives you placement options.

Your first background may or may not come out as hoped or expected, but it may work for a different project at a later date. Please remember to observe, relax and have fun. This is a creative process, which if you're reading this, you love!

Stitching a scene

Stitching a successful garden or meadow scene is dependent on building layers, first with paint, then stitches. Working over a painted background adds depth and interest, adding details that cannot be achieved with thread, as will varying the type of stitches used in the embroidery. Straight stitches will sit flat on the fabric, but looped and knotted stitches will sit up from the surface, creating small shadows and adding texture. Using various thread colours and weights and crossing stitches over and under one another will produce a more realistic result. When working with stranded cotton, increasing the number of strands will add weight to each stitched line.

These images follow the sequence from painting the first wash to the finished result.

1 / Apply a blue wash across the area, varying the depth of colour.

2 / Add a green wash across the lower section and wispy strands of grass.

3 / Work a background of dark, straight stiches with a heavier thread weight (three strands).

4 / Add lighter-coloured straight stitches, angling some slightly, to vary the background colour with a heavier thread weight (three strands).

5 / Add lighter-coloured, spaced straight stitches at varying angles, along the upper edge of the grassed area with a medium thread weight (two strands), blending the lower end of each stitch into the previous stitches.

6 / Add spaced straight stitches at varying angles with a lighter-coloured shade of green along the upper grassed area with a light thread weight (one strand), blending the lower ends of the stitches as before.

7 / Add spaced straight stitches at varying angles with another, lighter-coloured shade of green along the upper grassed area with a light thread weight (one strand), blending the lower ends of the stitches as before.

8 / Stitch the flowers, varying the size and thread weight and tucking some behind the light-coloured straight stitches.

9 / Add stems to most flowers with pistil stitch or straight stitch. It is not necessary to add a stem to every flower.

10 / Add stalks of wheat amongst the flowers. Look carefully at the composition and add straight stitches anywhere they are needed.

11 / Apply the mount to the finished embroidery.

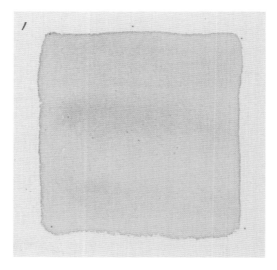

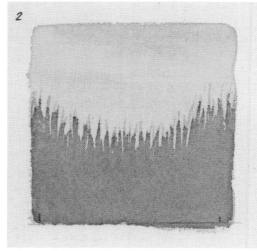

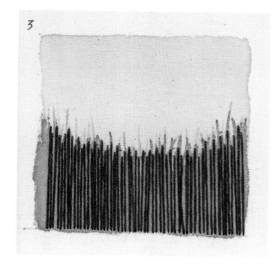

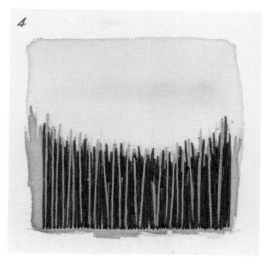

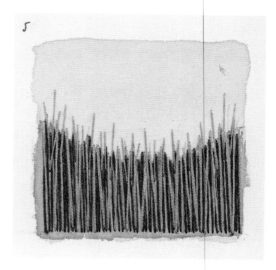

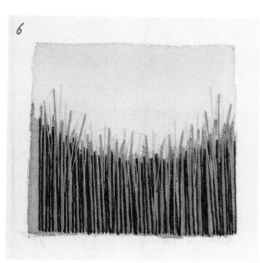

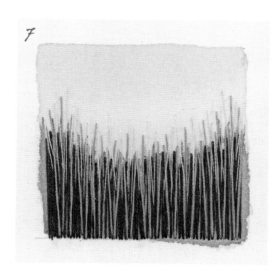

Seascape

The water greets the sky surrounded by cow parsley, daisies and a scattering of tiny flowers.

To see a World in a Grain of Sand
And a Heaven in a Wild Flower
Hold Infinity in the palm of your hand
And Eternity in an hour

William Blake

This Design Uses
Finger chain
Fly stitch
French knot
Pistil stitch
Straight stitch

The finished design measures
12cm x 29cm wide
(4 ¾" x 11½").

Requirements

Fabric

30cm x 50cm wide (12" x 20") piece of medium-weight calico (muslin)

Supplies

Slate frame or stretcher bars to fit fabric

Lacing thread (slate frame)

Thumb tacks (stretcher bars)

Cobalt blue watercolour

Yellow ochre watercolour

Palette or white plate

Large watercolour brush

Small watercolour brush

Masking tape

Ruler

25cm x 40cm wide (10" x 16") sheet of white paper

Paper scissors

Pins

HB pencil

Needles

No. 22 chenille

No. 5 crewel

No. 8 crewel

Threads & Ribbons

DMC stranded cotton

A = blanc

B = 23 apple blossom

C = 370 med verdigris

D = 524 vy lt fern green

E = 778 vy lt antique mauve

F = 936 dk avocado green

G = 963 ultra lt dusky rose

H = 3012 med khaki green

I = 3013 lt khaki green

J = 3820 dk straw

K = 3822 lt straw

Valdani no. 8 variegated perlé cotton

L = JP8 spring leaves

Di van Niekerk 2mm silk ribbon

M = 32 sunny green

N = 103 white

Preparation for Embroidery

Preparing the fabric

Using the ruler and pencil, lightly mark the corners of a 20cm x 35cm wide (8" x 14") rectangle at the centre of the calico. Mix a small amount of cobalt blue watercolour with water on the palette and apply a blue wash to the marked rectangle with the large brush, leaving small patches without paint to create clouds and texture in the sea. Allow to dry and press with an iron and pressing cloth. Measure down approximately one third from the upper edge of the rectangle and apply a line of masking tape to the painted fabric. The lower edge of the tape will be the horizon line. Mix a slightly darker blue wash for the sea, adding a little yellow if desired to create a slightly greener blue. Apply the wash over the lower section of the fabric with the large brush, up to and along the masking tape and over the initial blue wash. Allow to dry, remove the masking tape and press.

Mix a small amount of yellow ochre with the remaining blue paint to create green. Add more water if necessary to create a green wash. Using the small brush, paint in wispy grass along the base, making it higher at the sides of the rectangle (fig 1).

Allow to dry on a flat surface. Press with an iron and pressing cloth.

At the centre of the sheet of paper, measure and mark a 12cm x 29cm wide (4¾" x 11½") rectangle. Carefully cut away the paper from inside the rectangle. Position the paper mount over the painted fabric, moving it to frame the most pleasing section. Take care to ensure that the grainlines remain parallel with the cut edges of the paper. Mark each corner with a pin and remove the paper. Using the ruler and pencil, measure out 5mm (³⁄₁₆") from the marked point on each side and mark in a rectangle. It should measure 13cm x 30cm wide (5⅛" x 12"). This is the area that will be embroidered. Mount the fabric into the frame ensuring that it is drum tight.

Refer to the close-up photograph for colour and stitch placement.

Use the no. 22 chenille needle for the perlé cotton and ribbon, the no. 5 crewel needle for three strands of thread and the no. 8 crewel for one or two strands of thread.

All embroidery is worked in the frame.

Order of work

Hint: As you work, position the paper mount over the embroidery and pin in place. Prop your work up and leave it for 15-20 minutes. When you return, look at your stitching and you will be able to see any areas that need additional work.

BACKGROUND GRASSES

Beginning at the base line and using three strands of **F**, work long straight stitches, varying the length of each stitch and making them approximately 3cm-4cm (1⅛"-1½") towards the ends of the rectangle, curving down to approximately 1cm-2cm (⅜"-¾") at the centre.

- - - - - - - - - - - - - - - - - - - -

NOTE: Work the stitches in the same manner as laid work, making the first long stitch from the base upwards then taking a small stitch across to the tip of the next blade of grass and working it towards the base (diag 1).

This reduces bulk on the back of the work and uses much less thread.

Repeat with three strands of **I**, crossing the threads over and under each other.

Using two strands of **C**, add longer stitches, crisscrossing the previous, beginning at the base and working stitches approximately 4cm-6cm long (1½"-2⅜") towards the ends of the rectangle, curving down to approximately 2cm-3cm (¾"-1⅛") at the centre. Using one strand of **C**, add some 6cm-8cm (2⅜"-3⅛") stitches on both sides.

Repeat this using two strands of **H** then two strands of **I**, crisscrossing the previous stitches and working up into the taller lengths. Repeat again using one strand of **D** and **I**.

COW PARSLEY

Work the stems and umbels with fly stitch using one strand of **H**, positioning the V of the stitch to form the umbel and working a long anchoring stitch. Work 5-6 straight stitches of varying lengths in each umbel. Stitch one or two of the umbels and stems and, when working the next flower head, take the thread beneath the previous stitches before anchoring it amongst the grasses (diag 2).

Work two short straight stitches beneath the umbel using the same thread. Stitch the flowers with clusters of French knots using two strands of **A**, two strands of **B** or one strand of **B** and **G** together in the needle.

SEEDED GRASS

Work each seed head with a finger chain using one strand of **C**, **D** and **H** and following the step-by-step instructions on page 132. Once the chain is secured, anchor the thread with a long stitch to form the stem.

DAISIES

Flowers

Work the small and medium flower petals with straight stitches radiating out from the centre of the flower using **A**. Stitch some daisies side on and some with the petals upturned. Embroider the small flowers with two strands of thread and 5-6 stitches and the medium flowers with three strands of thread and 6-7 stitches. Stitch the large daisies using **N** and 4-6 stitches. Using two strands of **K**, work the centres of the small flowers with a French knot and the medium flowers with a two wrap French knot. Work the centres of the large flowers with a three wrap French knot using **J** and **K**.

Stems

Work the stems on the upturned flowers with pistil stitch and some of the remaining daisies with a long, straight stitch using two strands of **H**, tucking the lower end of each stitch behind the existing stitches.

ADDITIONAL GRASSES

Using **L** and **M**, add straight stitches across the lower edge of the scene, working over and under the existing stitches.

SMALL FLOWERS

Scatter French knot flowers along the base of the design using two strands of **E**, **J**, **K** and one strand of **B** and **E** together in the needle.

FINISHING

Place the paper mount over the embroidery and check to ensure that the design is completed to your satisfaction. Work any additional grass that may be needed using one strand of **D** or **I** and working long, straight stitches overlapping or tucking beneath the existing stitching.

Hollyhocks

Elegant spires, in shades of dusky pink and soft green, stretch towards the sky.

"Flowers have an expression of countenance as much as men or animals. Some seem to smile some have a sad expression some are pensive and diffident others again are plain, honest and upright, like the broad-faced sunflower and hollyhock."

Henry Ward Beecher

This design uses
French knot
Straight stitch

The finished design measures 20cm x 10cm wide (8" x 4").

Requirements

Fabric

35cm x 25cm wide (14" x 10") piece of medium-weight calico (muslin)

Supplies

Slate frame or stretcher bars to fit fabric

Lacing thread (slate frame)

Thumb tacks (stretcher bars)

Cerulean blue watercolour

Cadmium yellow watercolour

Palette or white plate

Large watercolour brush

Small watercolour brush

Ruler

30cm x 20cm wide (12" x 8") sheet of white paper

Paper scissors

Pins

Tracing paper

Fine black pen

HB pencil

Needle

No. 8 crewel

Threads

A = 727 lt golden yellow

B = 963 ultra lt dusky rose

C = 3348 lt yellow-green

D = 3350 ultra dk dusky rose

E = 3363 med pine green

F = 3364 pine green

G = 3685 wine

H = 3731 vy dk dusky rose

I = 3733 dusky rose

Embroidery

Refer to the close-up photograph for colour and stitch placement.

All embroidery is worked in the frame.

Order of work

> *Hint:* As you work, position the paper mount over the embroidery and pin in place.
> Prop your work up and leave it for 15-20 minutes. When you return, look at your stitching and you will be able to see any areas that need additional work.

HOLLYHOCKS

Work the hollyhocks beginning from the left-hand side using the listed colours. Work all the flowers before adding the stems and leaves.

Embroider the inner colour of the petals first with two strands, working straight stitch radiating from the centre. Work the outer colour in a similar manner using two strands of thread and radiating from the edge of the inner colour. Embroider the pink buds with straight stitch or two-wrap French knots using two strands of thread. Stitch the centre of each open flower with a French knot and two strands of **A**, using a two-wrap knot on the larger flowers. Work the leaves and stems with straight stitch, radiating each leaf from a central point and using two strands of thread. Work the green buds with French knots using the same thread, increasing to two-wraps for the lower knots.

HOLLYHOCK 1: flowers - **B** and **I**, leaves and stems – **E**

HOLLYHOCK 2: flowers – **H** and **B**, leaves and stems – **F**

30

HOLLYHOCK 3: flowers – **G** and **D**, leaves and stems – **F**

HOLLYHOCK 4: flowers – **D** and **I**, leaves and stems – **E**

HOLLYHOCK 5: flowers – **I** and **B**, leaves and stems **F**

HOLLYHOCK 6: flowers – **G** and **H**, leaves and stems – **E**

HOLLYHOCK 7: flowers – **D** and **I**, leaves and stems – **F**

HOLLYHOCK 8: flowers – **I** and **B**, leaves and stems – **F**

HOLLYHOCK 9: flowers – **G** and **D**, leaves and stems – **E**

HOLLYHOCK 10: flowers – **D** and **I**, leaves and stems – **F**

HOLLYHOCK 11: flowers – **D** and **H**, leaves and stems – **E**

GRASSES

Work long straight stitches from the base line up to the lower leaves using two strands of **E**, tucking some stitches under and working some over the leaves. Repeat with two strands of **F** then two strands of **C**. Add taller blades of grass amongst the hollyhock spires using one strand of **C** and **F** and overlapping some flowers and leaves.

FINISHING

Place the paper mount over the embroidery and check to ensure that the design is completed to your satisfaction. Work any additional stitches that may be needed.

Bluebells Under the Birches

A carpet of pure, blue flowers spreads beneath a canopy of birch leaves.

The Bluebell is the sweetest flower
That waves in summer air:
Its blossoms have the mightiest power
To soothe my spirits care.

Emily Brontë

This Design Uses
Back stitch
Fly stitch
Seed stitch
Straight stitch
Whipped back stitch

The finished design measures
10cm x 20cm wide (4" x 8").

Requirements

Needles

No. 24 chenille

No. 5 crewel

No. 8 crewel

Threads & Ribbons

DMC stranded cotton

A = blanc

B = 02 tin

C = 11 lt tender green

D = 155 violet

E = 333 vy dk blue-violet

F = 648 lt beaver grey

G = 935 vy dk avocado green

H = 3347 med yellow-green

I = 3348 lt yellow-green

J = 3362 dk pine green

K = 3363 med pine green

L = 3364 pine green

M = 3787 dk Jacobean green

N = 3807 cornflower blue

Di van Niekerk 2mm silk ribbon

O = 24 lt pine

P = 96 deepest purple

Fabric

25cm x 35cm wide (10" x 14") piece of medium-weight calico (muslin)

Supplies

Slate frame or stretcher bars to fit fabric

Lacing thread (slate frame)

Thumbtacks (stretcher bars)

15cm x 25cm wide (6" x 10") piece of tear-away fabric stabiliser

Cerulean blue watercolour

Cadmium yellow watercolour

Palette or white plate

Large watercolour brush

Small watercolour brush

Ruler

20cm x 30cm wide (8" x 12") sheet of white paper

Paper scissors

Pins

Tracing paper

Fine black pen

HB pencil

Preparation for Embroidery

Preparing the fabric

Using the ruler and pencil, lightly mark the corners of a 15cm x 25cm wide (6" x 10") rectangle at the centre of the calico. Mix a small amount of cerulean blue watercolour with water on the palette and apply a blue wash to the marked rectangle. Allow to dry.

Mix a small amount of cadmium yellow with the remaining blue paint to create green. Add more water if necessary to create a green wash.

Apply the wash to the lower third of the rectangle.

Using the small brush paint wispy, irregular blades of grass into the sky.

Mix a second shade of green and paint a dappled leaf effect in the upper area using the two shades of green (fig 1).

Allow to dry on a flat surface. Press with an iron and pressing cloth.

At the centre of the sheet of paper, measure and mark a 10cm x 20cm wide (4" x 8") rectangle. Carefully cut away the paper from inside the rectangle. Position the paper mount over the painted fabric, moving it to frame the most pleasing section. Take care to ensure that the grainlines remain parallel with the cut edges of the paper. Mark each corner with a pin and remove the paper. Using the ruler and pencil, measure out 5mm (³⁄₁₆") from the marked point on each side and mark in a rectangle. It should measure 11cm x 21cm wide (4¼" x 8¼"). This is the area to be embroidered.

Transferring the design

Using the pencil, trace the trunk shaping and markings onto the tear-away stabiliser. Cut out the trunks, leaving them connected above the upper outline (diag 1).

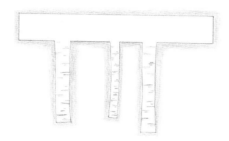

Position the trunks and hold in place with small stitches (fig 2).

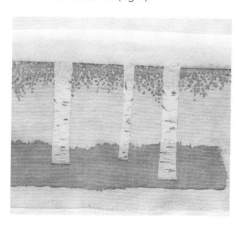

Using the fine black pen, transfer the design to the tracing paper. Tape the tracing to a lightbox or window. Position the fabric over the tracing, ensuring that the design is centred within the marked rectangle and the trunks are aligned. Lightly transfer the design using the HB pencil.

Mount the fabric into the frame ensuring it is drum tight.

Refer to the close-up photograph for colour and stitch placement.

Use the no. 24 chenille needle for the silk ribbon, the no. 5 crewel needle for three or four strands of thread and the no. 8 crewel for one or two strands of thread.

All embroidery is worked in the frame.

Order of work

Hint: As you work, position the paper mount over the embroidery and pin in place. Prop your work up and leave it for 15-20 minutes. When you return, look at your stitching and you will be able to see any areas that need additional work.

SILVER BIRCH

Trunk

Using two strands of **A**, work back stitch along the edge of the stabiliser on both sides of the left-hand trunk. Using the same thread, cover the trunk with horizontal straight stitches, working over the back stitch outline. Stitch the fissures in the bark with straight stitches of varying lengths using two strands of **F** and **M** and using the photographs as a guide to placement. Embroider the branches with whipped back stitch, using two strands of **M** for the large branches and one strand for the smaller ones. Work the right-hand trunk in the same manner.

Stitch the centre trunk in a similar manner, using two strands of **B** for the back stitch outline and horizontal straight stitches.

Leaves

Embroider the leaves with fly stitch, working the arms close together and using two strands of **H** then two strands of **I**. Add smaller leaves towards the tips of the branches using one strand of **H** and **I**. Work additional leaves across the upper half of the leaf area with two strands of **J**.

GRASSES

Fill the foreground with vertical straight stitches using two strands of **J**, varying the length by 1cm (³⁄₈") and making the stitches approximately 2cm-3cm long (³⁄₄"-1¹⁄₈"), increasing to 4cm (1½") and overlapping the tree trunk at the right-hand side of the rectangle.

Note: Work the stitches in the same manner as laid work, making the first long stitch from the base upwards then taking a small stitch across to the tip of the next blade of grass and working it towards the base (diag 2).

This reduces bulk on the back of the work and uses much less thread.

Add stitches using two strands of **G** to create an area of shade beneath the right-hand tree, overlapping and reaching up the trunk. Work an area of shade in the same manner beneath the left-hand tree using the same thread and shorter stitches. In the area between the shading and the base stitches, add straight stitches using two strands of **K**, merging them into the grasses above and below.

Work an area of shade beneath the centre tree with smaller straight stitches using two strands of **G**. Fill the areas on the outer sides of the tree trunks with layers of straight stitches of varying lengths using two strands of thread, beginning with **J** then **K** and finishing with **L**. Stitch the path through the centre of the design with straight stitches of varying lengths using two strands of **C**, **I** and **L**. Embroider the grasses on the

horizon with long straight stitches using one strand of **C** then repeat with one strand of **I** then one strand of **L**, varying the height and tucking the base of each stitch behind the existing stitches.

Add lighter grasses beneath the left and right-hand trees using two strands of **I** then one strand of **C**, crossing over the existing stitches.

BLUEBELLS

Work the bluebells in the background and beneath the left-hand and centre trees with seed stitch using two strands of **D**, **E** and **N** or a combination of two colours in the needle. Stitch the foreground flowers with small straight stitches using **P** and add straight stitch leaves around the flowers using **O**,

working at slight angles and crossing one another.

FINISHING

Place the paper mount over the embroidery and check to ensure that the design is completed to your satisfaction. Work any additional stitches that may be needed.

Topiary in
the Border

Perfect topiary spheres rise above a colourful sea of iris, geum, verbena and echinacea flowers.

"The love of gardening is a seed once sown that never dies."

Gertrude Jekyll

This Design Uses
Detached chain
Fly stitch
French knot
Straight stitch

The finished design measures 12cm (4 ¾") square.

Fabric

30cm (12") square of medium-weight calico (muslin)

Supplies

Slate frame or stretcher bars to fit fabric or 20cm (8") embroidery hoop

Lacing thread (slate frame)

Thumb tacks (stretcher bars)

10cm x 6cm wide (4" x 2 ½") piece of tear away fabric stabiliser

Cobalt blue watercolour

Cadmium yellow watercolour

Palette or white plate

Large watercolour brush

Small watercolour brush

Ruler

20cm (8") square of white paper

Paper scissors

Pins

HB pencil

Needles

No. 20 chenille

No. 24 chenille

No. 5 crewel

No. 8 crewel

Threads & Ribbons

DMC stranded cotton

A = 154 vy dk grape

B = 209 lavender

C = 603 cranberry

D = 728 vy dk golden yellow

E = 793 med cornflower blue

F = 936 dk avocado green

G = 3347 med yellow-green

H = 3348 lt yellow-green

I = 3350 ultra dk dusky rose

J = 3362 dk pine green

K = 3363 med pine green

L = 3364 pine green

M = 3685 wine

N = 3787 dk Jacobean green

O = 3853 dk autumn gold

P = 3854 med autumn gold

Di van Niekerk 2mm silk ribbon

Q = 19 fern

R = 64 hyacinth

Di van Niekerk 4mm silk ribbon

S = 53 dark peace rose

T = 54 buttercup

Preparing the fabric

Using the ruler and pencil, lightly mark the corners of a 20cm (8") square at the centre of the calico. Mix a small amount of cobalt blue watercolour with water on the palette and apply a blue wash to the marked square. Allow to dry.

Mix a small amount of cadmium yellow with the remaining blue paint to create green. Add more water if necessary to create a green wash. Apply the wash to the lower third of the rectangle. Using the small brush paint wispy, irregular blades of grass into the sky (fig 1).

Allow to dry on a flat surface. Press with an iron and pressing cloth.

Apply a green wash to the piece of fabric stabiliser and allow to dry.

At the centre of the sheet of paper, measure and mark a 12cm (4¾") square. Carefully cut away the paper from inside the square. Position the paper mount over the painted fabric, moving it to frame the most pleasing section. Take care to ensure that the grainlines remain parallel with the cut edges of the paper. Mark each corner with a pin and remove the paper. Using the ruler and pencil, measure out 5mm (³⁄₁₆") from the marked point on each side and mark in a square. It should measure 13cm (5⅛") square. This is the area that will be embroidered. At the centre of the base line measure and mark a 10cm (4") vertical line with the ruler and pencil.

Transferring the design

Using the black pen, trace the topiary shape and shading guidelines for the topiary balls onto the tracing paper.

Centre the coloured fabric stabiliser over the tracing and transfer the outline and shading guidelines. If desired, shade the topiary using green watercolour. Cut out around the outline. Centre the shape over the marked vertical line on the painted fabric with the lower edge approximately 3cm (1⅛") above the base line and hold in place with several small stitches (fig 2).

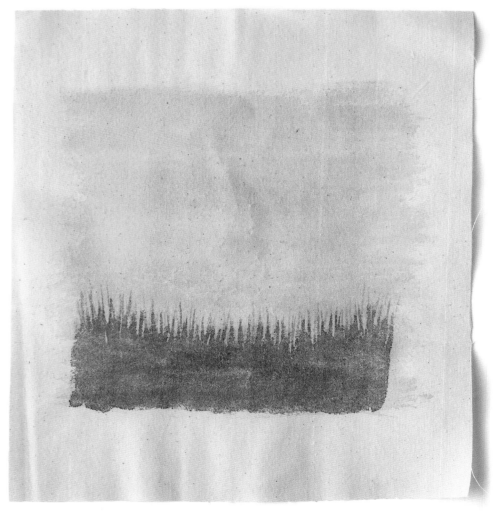

Mount the fabric into the frame or hoop ensuring that it is drum tight.

Embroidery

Refer to the close-up photograph for colour and stitch placement.

Use the no. 20 chenille needle for the 4mm ribbon, the no. 24 chenille for the 2mm ribbon, the no. 5 crewel needle for three or four strands of thread and the no. 8 crewel for one or two strands of thread.

All embroidery is worked in a frame or hoop.

Order of work

Hint: As you work, position the paper mount over the embroidery and pin in place. Prop your work up and leave it for 15-20 minutes. When you return, look at your stitching and you will be able to see any areas that need additional work.

TOPIARY

Using the marked lines as a guide, fill each ball with two-wrap French knots using two strands of thread, blending the colours at the edge of each band to avoid lines.

Begin at the top of the ball with two strands of **L**, blending into two strands of **K** in the centre section then two strands of **J** in the lower section, taking care not to create a solid line around the outer edge.

GRASSES

Beginning at the base line and using three strands of **F**, cover the base of the green area with vertical straight stitches, varying the length of each stitch slightly, making the stitches approximately 3cm-4cm long (1⅛"-1½") and overlapping the base of the topiary.

Note: Work the stitches in the same manner as laid work, making the first long stitch from the base upwards then taking a small stitch across to the tip of the next blade of grass and working it towards the base (diag 1).

This reduces bulk on the back of the work and uses much less thread.

Repeat this process using three strands of **K**, filling any gaps.

Working across the top of the base grasses and overlapping the base of the topiary, add more grass to the foreground, beginning with two strands

of **H** then one strand of **G** and finishing with one strand of **F**.

GEUM

Work each geum flower above the dark grasses with straight stitches, radiating from the centre and using two strands of **O** for some flowers and two strands of **P** for the remainder. Using **L**, add stems and some additional 1cm-2cm (⅜"-¾") grasses with straight stitch on the green painted area, tucking the base of the stitches behind the base grasses and leaving gaps to soften the skyline.

VERBENA

Work the umbels and stems with fly stitch using one strand of **G** and tucking them around and under the geums into the base grasses. Stitch one or two of the umbels and stems and, when working the next flower head, take the thread beneath the previous stitches before anchoring it amongst the grasses (diag 2).

Stitch the flowers with 5-7 French knots in each umbel, using one strand of **A** and **B** together in the needle for some plants and one strand of **B** and **E** together in the needle for the remainder.

ECHINACEA

Embroider the flowers across the dark grass area, varying the size and working 5-8 radiating straight stitches for each flower head. Vary the colours of the flowers using the following threads together in the needle: two strands of **C** and one of **I**, two strands of **I** and one of **M** or two strands of **M** and one of **I**.

Stitch the centre of each flower with a two-wrap French knot using two strands of **D** and one strand of **N** together in the needle.

IRIS

Each iris is worked with detached chain and ribbon stitch emanating from a centre point and using **R**, **S** and **T**. Stitch the detached chain first, one upwards and one downwards then add the ribbon stitches, angling them down slightly. Take care not to pull the stitches tightly as the ribbon should sit up on the fabric creating a three-dimensional

effect. Embroider each bud with a straight stitch, worked at an angle and using the same ribbons. Work the stems using **Q**, bringing the ribbon to the surface at the base of the stem and twisting it firmly before taking it to the back at the base of the lower petal. Allow the ribbon to untwist on the back of the work before stitching the next stem. Using the same ribbon, work a fly stitch around each bud, anchoring the stitch next to the stem. Using **Q**, add leaves with long, straight stitches

worked at slight angles and crossing over or under the previous stitching.

FOREGROUND GRASSES

Work additional long, straight stitches using one or two strands of **H** to ensure that all elements are naturally integrated.

FINISHING

Place the paper mount over the embroidery and check to ensure that the design is completed to your satisfaction. Work any additional stitches that may be needed.

Amongst the Daisies

A field of fresh, white daisies, some crowned with
a golden eye, spread beneath the sun.

> *Where innocent bright-eyed daisies are*
> *With blades of grass between,*
> *Each daisy stands up like a star*
> *Out of a sky of green.*

Christina Rossetti

This Design Uses
Detached blanket stitch
French knot
Pistil stitch
Straight stitch

The finished design
measures 12cm x 29cm wide
(4¾" x 11½").

Requirements

Fabric

30cm x 50cm wide (12" x 20") piece of medium-weight calico (muslin)

Supplies

Slate frame or stretcher bars to fit fabric

Lacing thread (slate frame)

Thumb tacks (stretcher bars)

Cobalt blue watercolour

Cadmium yellow watercolour

Palette or white plate

Large watercolour brush

Ruler

25cm x 40cm wide (10" x 16") sheet of white paper

Paper scissors

Pins

HB pencil

Needles

No. 5 crewel

No. 8 crewel

Threads

DMC stranded cotton

A = blanc

B = 17 lt yellow plum

C = 727 lt golden yellow

D = 728 vy dk golden yellow

E = 772 vy lt yellow-green

F = 935 vy dk avocado green

G = 3053 green-grey

H = 3348 lt yellow-green

I = 3362 dk pine green

Preparing the fabric

Using the ruler and pencil, lightly mark the corners of a 20cm x 40cm wide (8" x 16") rectangle at the centre of the calico. Mix a small amount of cobalt blue watercolour with water on the palette and apply a blue wash to the marked rectangle, leaving small patches without paint in the upper half to create clouds. Allow to dry slightly.

Mix a small amount of cadmium yellow with the remaining blue paint to create green. Add more water if necessary to create a green wash. Apply the wash to the lower section of the rectangle. As the blue is still damp, the green should bleed into it, creating a hazy line where the colours intersect (fig 1).

Allow to dry on a flat surface. Press with an iron and pressing cloth.

At the centre of the sheet of paper, measure and mark a 12cm x 29cm wide (4¾" x 11½") rectangle. Carefully cut away the paper from inside the rectangle. Position the paper mount over the painted fabric, moving it to frame the most pleasing section. Take care to ensure that the grainlines remain parallel with the cut edges of the paper. Mark each corner with a pin and remove the paper. Using the ruler and pencil, measure out 5mm (³⁄₁₆") from the marked point on each side and mark in a rectangle. It should measure 13cm x 30cm wide (5⅛" x 12"). This is the area that will be embroidered. Mount the fabric into the frame ensuring that it is drum tight.

Embroidery

Refer to the close-up photograph for colour and stitch placement.

Use the no. 5 crewel needle for three or four strands of thread and the no. 8 crewel for one or two strands of thread.

All embroidery is worked in the frame.

Order of work

Hint: As you work, position the paper mount over the embroidery and pin in place. Prop your work up and leave it for 15-20 minutes. When you return, look at your stitching and you will be able to see any areas that need additional work.

BACKGROUND GRASSES

Beginning at the base line and using three strands of **F**, cover the lower half of the green area with vertical straight stitches, varying the length of each stitch slightly and making them 6cm-7cm long (2⅜"-2¾") towards the ends of the rectangle, curving down to 5cm-6cm long (2"-2⅜") at the centre.

- - - - - - - - - - - - - - - - - - -

Note: Work the stitches in the same manner as laid work, making the first long stitch from the base upwards then taking a small stitch across to the tip of the next blade of grass and working it towards the base (diag 1).

This reduces bulk on the back of the work and uses much less thread.

Repeat this process using three strands of **I**, filling any gaps.

Using two strands of **I**, work another layer of spaced straight stitches, extending them 2cm (¾") past the first layers at the upper edge and tucking the lower ends behind the existing stitches. Repeat this process using two strands of **G**, crossing the previous layer. Using the photograph as a guide and one strand of **G** and **H**, work longer straight stitches across the horizon,

making them approximately 4cm-6cm (1½"-2⅜") towards the ends and 2cm-3cm (¾"-1⅛") at the centre, tucking the lower ends behind the existing stitches.

DAISIES

Flowers

The petals are worked with straight stitches radiating out from the centre of the flower using **A**. Work some daisies with a full face, some side on and some with the petals upturned. Work the

small, background flowers with two strands of thread and 4-5 stitches, the medium, mid-ground flowers with three strands of thread and 6-7 stitches and the large, foreground flowers with four strands of thread and 7-9 stitches. Stitch the centres of the small flowers with a French knot using two strands of **C**, the medium flowers with a one or two wrap French knot using two strands of **B** and the large flowers with a two or three wrap French knot using two strands of **D**.

Stems

Work the stems on most flowers with straight stitch or pistil stitch using **E**, **G** and **H**, using one strand for the small and medium daisies and two strands for the large daisies, tucking the lower end of each stitch behind the existing stitches.

ADDITIONAL GRASSES

Embroider additional straight stitch grass stems over the background using one strand of **E**, **G** and **H** and working over and under the daisies. Using the same threads add straight stitches to the foreground in the same manner using one strand then repeat with two strands of thread.

SEEDED GRASS

The seed heads are worked with detached blanket stitch using two strands of **E** and **H**. Work the straight stitch foundation approximately 1cm (⅜") long and cover with detached blanket stitch, anchoring the thread at the base of the stalk.

FINISHING

Place the paper mount over the embroidery and check to ensure that the design is completed to your satisfaction. Work any additional stitches that may be needed.

Irises

Rich, velvety petals of the purple iris rise above a sea of sword-like leaves.

"What in your life is calling you, When all the noise is silenced, The meetings adjourned... The lists laid aside, And the Wild Iris blooms By itself In the dark forest... What still pulls on your soul?"

Rumi

This Design Uses
Detached chain
Ribbon stitch
Straight stitch

The finished design measures 12cm (4¾") square.

IRISES

Requirements

Fabric

30cm (12") square of medium-weight calico (muslin)

Supplies

Slate frame or stretcher bars to fit fabric or 20cm (8") embroidery hoop

Lacing thread (slate frame)

Thumb tacks (stretcher bars)

Ultramarine blue watercolour

Cadmium yellow watercolour

Palette or white plate

Large watercolour brush

Ruler

20cm (8") square of white paper

Paper scissors

Pins

HB pencil

Needles

No. 18 chenille

No. 20 chenille

No. 5 crewel

No. 8 crewel

Threads

DMC stranded cotton

 A = 11 lt tender green

 B = 935 vy dk avocado green

 C = 3012 med khaki green

 D = 3013 lt khaki green

 E = 3348 lt yellow-green

Di van Niekerk 4mm silk ribbon

 F = 19 fern

Di van Niekerk 7mm silk ribbon

 G = 15 grey-green

 H = 73 lilac dazzle

 I = 96 deepest purple

Preparation for Embroidery

Preparing the fabric

Using the ruler and pencil, lightly mark the corners of a 20cm (8") square at the centre of the calico. Mix a small amount of cadmium yellow watercolour with water on the palette and apply a yellow wash to the marked square. Allow to dry slightly.

Mix a small amount of ultramarine blue with the remaining yellow paint to create green. Add more water if necessary to create a green wash. Apply the wash to the lower half of the square with vertical brush strokes and dab the paint onto the upper half with the tip of the brush. The paint should bleed slightly as the fabric is still damp. Allow to dry a little more then add dabs of strong yellow to the upper half, aiming for a camouflage effect (fig 1).

Allow to dry on a flat surface. Press with an iron and pressing cloth.

At the centre of the sheet of paper, measure and mark a 12cm (4¾") square. Carefully cut away the paper from inside the square. Position the paper mount over the painted fabric, moving it to frame the most pleasing section. Take care to ensure that the grainlines remain parallel with the cut edges of the paper. Mark each corner with a pin and remove the paper. Using the ruler and pencil, measure out 5mm (³⁄₁₆") from the marked point on each side and mark in a square. It should measure 13cm (5⅛") square. This is the area that will be embroidered.

Mount the fabric into the frame or hoop ensuring that it is drum tight.

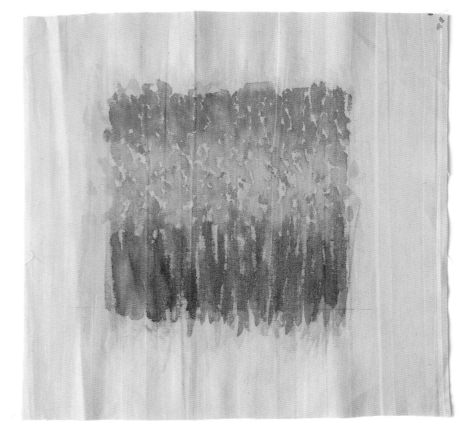

Embroidery

Refer to the close-up photograph for colour and stitch placement.

Use the no. 18 chenille needle for the 7mm ribbon, the no. 20 chenille for the 4mm ribbon, the no. 5 crewel needle for three strands of thread and the no. 8 crewel for one strand of thread.

All embroidery is worked in a frame or hoop.

Order of work

Hint: As you work, position the paper mount over the embroidery and pin in place. Prop your work up and leave it for 15-20 minutes. When you return, look at your stitching and you will be able to see any areas that need additional work.

BACKGROUND GRASSES

Beginning at the base line and using three strands of **B**, cover the lower third of the square with vertical straight stitches, varying the length by 1cm (⅜").

NOTE: Work the stitches in the same manner as laid work, making the first long stitch from the base upwards then taking a small stitch across to the tip of the next blade of grass and working it towards the base (diag 1).

This reduces bulk on the back of the work and uses much less thread.

Repeat this process using three strands of **C**, crossing the previous stitches and filling any gaps.

Using one strand of **A**, work a layer of spaced straight stitches, working stitches 3cm-4cm (1⅛"-1½") in length from amongst the existing stitches and creating an uneven upper edge. Repeat this process using one strand of **C** then **D**.

IRIS

Flowers

Each iris is worked with detached chain, a looped straight stitch and ribbon stitches using **H** and **I** and following the step-by-step instructions on page 71. Take care not to pull the stitches tightly as the ribbon should sit up on the fabric creating a three-dimensional effect.

Buds

Work each bud with an angled straight stitch using **H** and **I**.

Stems

Work the stems using **F**, bringing the ribbon to the surface at the base of the stem and twisting it firmly before taking it to the back at the base of the lower petal. Allow the ribbon to untwist on the back of the work before stitching the next stem. Using the same ribbon, work a detached chain on each side of each bud, twisting the ribbon tightly before anchoring the stitch to form the bud stem on one detached chain.

Leaves

Using **F**, add leaves with long, straight stitches worked at slight angles and crossing over the previous stitching. Work the foreground leaves in the same manner using **G**.

FINISHING

Place the paper mount over the embroidery and check to ensure that the design is completed to your satisfaction. Work any additional stitches that may be needed.

SILK RIBBON IRIS

These beautiful irises are formed with detached chain, looped straight stitch and ribbon stitches using hand-painted, 7mm silk ribbon. Take care not to pull the ribbon too tightly so that it forms broad, plump petals.

1 / Emerge at A and embroider a detached chain upwards.

2 / Emerge as close to A as possible and embroider a detached chain downwards, making it the same size as the previous stitch.

3 / Bring the ribbon to the front at the right of the top of the upper detached chain.

4 / Using the eye of the needle, take the ribbon behind the top of the lower detached chain.

5 / Take the ribbon to the back to the left of the top of the upper detached chain and pull through to complete the looped stitch.

6 / Carefully bring the ribbon to the front between the base of the upper detached chain and the looped stitch on one side of the flower centre.

7 / Work a ribbon stitch, angling it down slightly.

8 / Repeat steps 6-7 on the remaining side of the flower.

Cottage
Garden

Swathes of flowers, large and small, meld together in perfect harmony.

"Nothing is more completely the child of art than a garden."

Walter Scott

This Design Uses
Back stitch
Detached chain
Fly stitch
French knot
Satin stitch
Straight stitch
Whipped back stitch

The finished design measures
12cm x 29cm wide (4¾" x 11½").

Fabric

30cm x 50cm wide (12" x 20") piece of medium-weight calico (muslin)

Supplies

Slate frame or stretcher bars to fit fabric

Lacing thread (slate frame)

Thumb tacks (stretcher bars)

Ultramarine blue watercolour

Cadmium yellow watercolour

Palette or white plate

Large watercolour brush

Small watercolour brush

Ruler

25cm x 40cm wide (10" x 16") sheet of white paper

Paper scissors

Pins

Tracing paper

Fine black pen

HB pencil

Needles

No. 5 crewel

No. 8 crewel

Threads

DMC stranded cotton

A = blanc

B = 03 med tin

C = 12 tender green

D = 17 lt yellow plum

E = 29 eggplant

F = 210 med lavender

G = 340 med blue-violet

H = 341 lt blue violet

I = 522 fern green

J = 792 dk cornflower blue

K = 793 med cornflower blue

L = 794 lt cornflower blue

M = 935 vy dk avocado green

N = 963 ultra lt dusky rose

O = 3078 vy lt golden yellow

P = 3347 med yellow-green

Q = 3350 ultra dk dusky rose

R = 3354 lt dusky rose

S = 3362 dk pine green

T = 3363 med pine green

U = 3364 pine green

V = 3731 vy dk dusky rose

W = 3733 dusky rose

Preparation for Embroidery

Preparing the fabric

Using the ruler and pencil, lightly mark the corners of a 20cm x 40cm wide (8" x 16") rectangle at the centre of the calico. Mix a small amount of ultramarine blue watercolour with water on the palette and, using the large brush, apply a blue wash to the marked rectangle, leaving small patches without paint in the upper half to create clouds. Allow to dry.

Mix a small amount of cadmium yellow with the remaining blue paint to create green. Add more water if necessary to create a green wash. Apply the wash to the lower third of the rectangle. Using the small brush, paint wispy, irregular blades of grass into the sky (fig 1).

Allow to dry on a flat surface. Press with an iron and pressing cloth.

At the centre of the sheet of paper, measure and mark a 12cm x 29cm wide (4¾" x 11½") rectangle. Carefully cut away the paper from inside the rectangle. Position the paper mount over the painted fabric, moving it to frame the most pleasing section. Take care to ensure that the grainlines remain parallel with the cut edges of the paper. Mark each corner with a pin and remove the paper. Using the ruler and pencil, measure out 5mm (³⁄₁₆") from the marked point on each side and mark in a rectangle. It should measure 13cm x 30cm wide (5⅛" x 12"). This is the area that will be embroidered.

Transferring the design

Using the black pen, transfer the design and outline onto the tracing paper. Tape the tracing to a lightbox or window. Position the fabric over the tracing, aligning the marked rectangles and tape in place. Transfer the design using the pencil.

Mount the fabric into the frame ensuring that it is drum tight.

Embroidery

Refer to the close-up photograph for colour and stitch placement.

Use the no. 5 crewel needle for three or four strands of thread and the no. 8 crewel for one or two strands of thread.

All embroidery is worked in the frame.

Order of work

Hint: As you work, position the paper mount over the embroidery and pin in place. Prop your work up and leave it for 15-20 minutes. When you return, look at your stitching and you will be able to see any areas that need additional work.

BIRD TABLE

Outline the post, base and walls of the table with back stitch using one strand of **A**. Using two strands of the same thread, cover the post, walls and base with satin stitch. Work the supports between the base and pole with straight stitch using the same thread.

Outline the roof and tile sections with back stitch using one strand of **B**. Cover each section with satin stitch using two strands of the same thread. Outline the finial with back stitch using one strand of **A** and cover with satin stitch using two strands of the same thread.

ROSE OBELISK

Obelisk

Using two strands of **A**, embroider the outer and central supports with whipped back stitch. Work the inner supports in the same manner using one strand of **A**.

Stitch the finial in the same manner as the bird table.

Rose

Embroider the flowers with one or two-wrap French knots using two strands of **D**. Stitch the leaves with small straight stitches using two strands of **T** and the stems with straight stitch using one strand of **M**, linking the leaves and working around the supports.

BASE GRASSES

Beginning at the base line and using three strands of **M**, cover the base of the green area with vertical straight stitches, varying the length of each stitch slightly and making them 4cm-5cm (1½"-2") in length.

NOTE: Work the stitches in the same manner as laid work, making the first long stitch from the base upwards then taking a small stitch across to the tip of the next blade of grass and working it towards the base (diag 1).

This reduces bulk on the back of the work and uses much less thread.

Repeat this process using three strands of **S**, crossing the previous stitches and filling any gaps.

Working above the darker grasses, embroider straight stitches in a similar manner across the rectangle using two strands of **S**, making the stitches 1cm-2cm (⅜"-¾") in length and leaving gaps to soften the skyline. Tuck the ends behind the existing stitches.

HOLLYHOCKS

Work the hollyhocks beginning from the left-hand side using the listed colours.

Embroider the flower petals with one strand of each colour together in the needle, working straight stitch radiating from the centre for the open flowers and French knots for the pink buds. When stitching hollyhock 6, work the upper flowers with a small circle of

straight stitch at the centre using one strand of **Q** before stitching the petals. Stitch the leaves and stems with straight stitch, radiating each leaf from a central point and using two strands of thread. Work the green buds with French knots using the same thread.

HOLLYHOCK 1: flowers – **Q** and **W**, leaves and stems – **T**

HOLLYHOCK 2: flowers – **R** and **V**, leaves and stems – **U**

HOLLYHOCK 3: flowers – **N** and **R**, leaves and stems – **T**

HOLLYHOCK 4: flowers – **Q** and **W**, leaves and stems – **T**

HOLLYHOCK 5: flowers – **R** and **V**, leaves and stems **U**

HOLLYHOCK 6: flowers – two strands of **W**, leaves and stems – **T**

HOLLYHOCK 7: flowers – **R** and **V**, leaves and stems – **U**

HOLLYHOCK 8: flowers – **N** and **R**, leaves and stems – **T**

Fill the centre of each flower with a French knot using **D**.

SALVIA

Using one strand of **H** and **J** together in the needle, work each flower spike with 10-13 French knots. Stitch the stems with straight stitches using one strand of **M**.

ANGELICA

Fill each flower head with clusters of French knots, using two strands of **C** in the upper section and blending into one strand of **C** and **P** together in the needle for the lower section. Work each stem with a long straight stitch using two strands of **P** and stitch the leaves with detached chain using the same thread.

MID-GROUND GRASSES

Add a mid-ground layer of grasses between the hollyhocks and delphiniums, working the long straight stitches up and under the plants that have been stitched using two strands of **S**.

FOXGLOVES

Work the foxgloves beginning from the left-hand side and using the listed colours.

Begin at the top of each stem and work the pink buds with French knots using the first flower colour, changing to two-wrap knots as you come down the stem. Embroider the flower petals with two strands, working a detached chain using the first colour then a straight stitch through the centre of the chain using the second colour. Stitch the leaves with detached chain using two or three strands of thread and work the stems with straight stitch using two strands of thread. Stitch the green buds with French knots using two strands of the same thread.

FOXGLOVE 1: flowers – **Q** and **V**, leaves and stems **T**

FOXGLOVE 2: flowers – **R** and **N**, leaves and stems – **I**

FOXGLOVE 3: flowers – two strands of **W**, leaves and stems – **T**

FOXGLOVE 4: flowers – **N** and **V**, leaves and stems – **I**

FOXGLOVE 5: flowers – **N** and **W**, leaves and stems – **T**

FOXGLOVE 6: flowers – **W** and **V**, leaves and stems – **I**

FOXGLOVE 7: flowers – **Q** and **V**, leaves and stems – **T**

FOXGLOVE 8: flowers – **W** and **V**, leaves and stems – **T**

FOXGLOVE 9: flowers – **R** and **N**, leaves and stems – **I**

FOXGLOVE 10: flowers – **W** and **Q**, leaves and stems – **T**

COW PARSLEY

Using one strand of **T** for some and **U** for the remainder, work the stems and umbels with fly stitch and straight stitch (diag 2).

Tuck them in behind the foxgloves and bird table. Stitch the flowers with French knots using one strand of **A**.

DELPHINIUMS

Work the delphiniums beginning from the left-hand side and using the listed colours. Begin at the top of the stem and work the straight stitch buds using two strands of thread, working one stitch at the top of the stem and changing to two stitches as the buds become larger. Stitch the flowers with five straight stitches radiating from the centre. Work each centre with a French knot using two strands of thread.

DELPHINIUM 1: petals – **H**, centre – **E**

DELPHINIUM 2: petals – **L**, centre – **J**

DELPHINIUM 3: petals – **J**, centre – **A**

DELPHINIUM 4: petals – **K**, centre – **J**

DELPHINIUM 5: petals – **H**, centre – **E**

DELPHINIUM 6: petals – **L**, centre – **J**

DELPHINIUM 7: petals – **J**, centre – **A**

All leaves and stems are worked with straight stitch using **P** with one strand for the stems and two strands for the leaves.

IRIS

Work the flower petals with detached chain using two strands of **F** and **G** or **F** and **H** together in the needle. Work each bud with a single detached chain using the same threads and surround each one with a fly stitch using two strands of **I**, extending the anchoring

stitch to create the bud stem. Embroider the remaining stems with straight stitch using the same thread.

NIGELLA

Using one strand of **H** and **K** or one strand of **J** and **K** together in the needle, work the flowers with French knots or 3-4 straight stitches. Stitch the stems with straight stitch using one strand of **P**.

ENGLISH LAVENDER

Work the flower heads with straight stitch using two strands of **F**, **H** or one strand of **F** and **H** or one strand of **E** and **H** together in the needle, working the different colours randomly across the area. Embroider the stems with straight stitch using one strand of **I**.

PINK DAISIES

Using two strands of **R** for some flowers and one strand of **R** and **N** together in the needle for the remainder, work each flower with straight stitch radiating from the centre. Stitch the centres with a French knot using two strands of **E**. Work the stems with straight stitch using one strand of **U** and two strands of **I**.

YELLOW DAISIES

Stitch the yellow daisies in the same manner as the pink, using two strands of **D** and **O** for the petals and two strands of **E** for the centres. Work the stems with straight stitch using one strand of **T**.

ACHILLEA

Using one strand of **C**, work the stems and umbels with fly stitch, tucking the ends beneath the existing stitches. Stitch the flowers with French knots using two strands of the same thread.

PENSTEMON

Embroider the penstemons in the same manner as the foxgloves, using two strands of **Q** or one strand of **E** and **Q** together in the needle for the buds and flowers and two strands of **U** for the leaves and green buds.

GRASSES

To naturalise and merge the various plants and to ensure there are no gaps in the border, add extra grasses using one strand of a variety of greens, overlapping and tucking the stitches behind the existing work.

BEES

Scatter bees amongst the flowers, working each body with a French knot using **D** and **E** together in the needle and hinting at the wings with a French knot worked above the body using one strand of **E**.

FINISHING

Place the paper mount over the embroidery and check to ensure that the design is completed to your satisfaction. Work any additional stitches that may be needed.

Alliums & Topiary

Globes of purple allium flowers echo the neatly clipped sphere of a topiary ball.

"In my garden there is a large place for sentiment. My garden of flowers is also my garden of thoughts and dreams. The thoughts grow as freely as the flowers, and the dreams are as beautiful."

Abram L. Urban

This Design Uses
Fly stitch
French knot
Straight stitch
Whipped back stitch
Whipped chain stitch

The finished design measures 14cm (5½") square.

Small watercolour brush
Ruler
20cm (8") square of white paper
Paper scissors
Pins
Tracing paper
Fine black pen
HB pencil

Needles

No. 5 crewel
No. 8 crewel

Threads

DMC stranded cotton

A = blanc

B = 14 pale apple green

C = 32 dk blueberry

D = 208 dk lavender

E = 209 lavender

F = 210 med lavender

G = 211 lt lavender

H = 333 vy dk blue-violet

I = 934 black avocado green

J = 3348 lt yellow-green

K = 3362 dk pine green

L = 3363 med pine green

M = 3364 pine green

N = 3787 dk Jacobean green

Fabric

30cm (12") square of medium-weight calico (muslin)

Supplies

Slate frame, stretcher bars to fit fabric or a 25cm (10") embroidery hoop

Lacing thread (slate frame)

Thumbtacks (stretcher bars)

10cm (4") square of tear away fabric stabiliser

Cobalt blue watercolour

Cadmium yellow watercolour

Palette or white plate

Large watercolour brush

Preparation for Embroidery

Preparing the fabric

Using the ruler and pencil, lightly mark the corners of a 20cm (8") square at the centre of the calico. Mix a small amount of cobalt blue watercolour with water on the palette and apply a blue wash to the marked square. Allow to dry.

Mix a small amount of cadmium yellow with the remaining blue paint to create green. Add more water if necessary to create a green wash. Apply the wash to approximately the lower third of the square. Using the small brush paint wispy, irregular blades of grass into the sky, making them slightly higher at the ends (fig 1).

Allow to dry on a flat surface. Press with an iron and pressing cloth.

Apply a green wash to the square of fabric stabiliser and allow to dry.

At the centre of the sheet of paper, measure and mark a 14cm (5½") square. Carefully cut away the paper from inside the square. Position the paper mount over the painted fabric, moving it to frame the most pleasing section. Take care to ensure that the grainlines remain parallel with the cut edges of the paper. Mark each corner with a pin and remove the paper. Using the ruler and pencil, measure out 5mm (³⁄₁₆") from the marked point on each side

and mark in a square. It should measure 15cm (6") square. This is the area that will be embroidered. At the centre of the base line, measure and mark a 10cm (4") vertical line with the ruler and pencil.

Transferring the design

Using the black pen, trace the circles and shading guidelines for the alliums and topiary ball onto the tracing paper.

Centre the coloured square of fabric stabiliser over the topiary tracing and transfer the outline and shading guidelines. If desired, shade the topiary using green watercolour. Cut out around the outline. Centre the circle over the top of the marked vertical line on the painted fabric with the lower edge approximately 7cm (2¾") above the base line and hold in place with several small stitches (fig 2).

Tape the tracing to a lightbox or window. Position the fabric over the tracing, aligning the topiary circle and the straight grain with the stem lines and tape in place. Lightly transfer the allium outlines, shading guidelines and stem lines onto the fabric with the HB pencil.

Mount the fabric into the frame or hoop ensuring that it is drum tight.

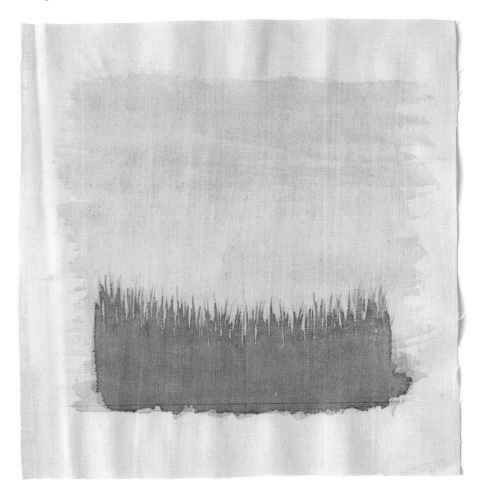

Embroidery

Refer to the close-up photograph for colour and stitch placement.

Use the no. 5 crewel needle for three or four strands of thread and the no. 8 crewel for one or two strands of thread.

All embroidery is worked in a frame or hoop.

Order of work

> *Hint:* As you work, position the paper mount over the embroidery and pin in place. Prop your work up and leave it for 15-20 minutes. When you return, look at your stitching and you will be able to see any areas that need additional work.

TOPIARY

Stem

Work the stem with whipped chain stitch using two strands of **N**, beginning amongst the painted grass and finishing just within the stabiliser circle.

Foliage

Using the marked lines as a guide, fill the ball with two-wrap French knots using two strands of thread, blending the colours at the edge of each band to avoid lines.

Begin at the top of the ball and fill each section with the following colours.

BAND 1: **L**, **M**, one strand of **B** and **M** together in the needle

BAND 2: **K**, **L** and **M**

BAND 3: **I**, **K** and **L**

BAND 4: **I** and **K**

ALLIUMS

Stems

Work the stems with whipped back stitch using two strands of **M**.

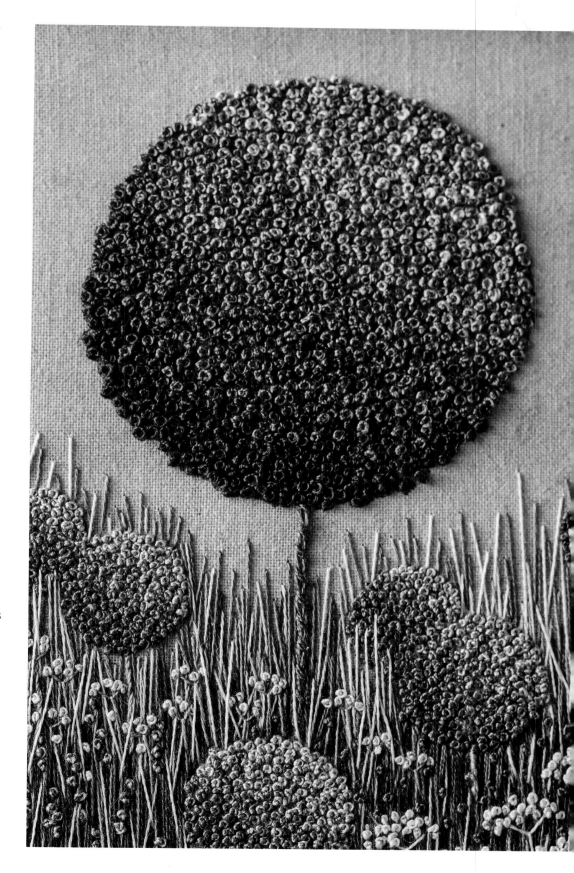

Flower heads

Using the marked lines as a guide, fill each flower head with French knots using two strands of thread, blending the colours at the edge of each band to prevent lines. Begin at the top of each ball and fill each section with the following colours.

BAND 1: **G**

BAND 2: **F**

BAND 3: **E**

BAND 4: **D**

Where the flower heads overlap, add knots with two strands of **C** to create a shaded area at the base of the background flower head (diag 1).

GRASSES

Beginning at the base line and using three strands of **I**, cover the base of the green area with vertical straight stitches, varying the length of each stitch slightly and making the stitches approximately 4cm-5cm long (1½-2"). Work the stitches around and behind the alliums and overlap the topiary stem in some areas.

- - - - - - - - - - - - - - - - - - - -

Note: Work the stitches in the same manner as laid work, making the first long stitch from the base upwards then taking a small stitch across to the tip of the next blade of grass and working it towards the base (diag 1).

This reduces bulk on the back of the work and uses much less thread.

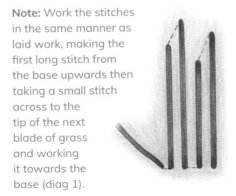

Repeat this process using three strands of **L**, filling any gaps.

Add a further layer of grasses above the previous, varying the lengths, crossing the stitches, tucking the lower ends behind the existing stitches and using one strand of **B**, **J**, **L** and **M**. Use only **L** and **M** beneath the topiary to create an area of shade.

ACHILLEA

Work the umbels and stems on the right-hand side with fly stitch using one strand of **B** and tucking the ends of the stems behind the existing stitches. Embroider the flowers with clusters of French knots using one strand of **A** and **B** together in the needle or two strands of **B**. Work the smaller achillea on the left-hand side and towards the centre in a similar manner, using one strand of **M** for the fly stitch and one strand of **B** and **G** together in the needle for the flowers.

LAVENDER

Stitch the flowers with irregular columns of French knots using one strand of **E** and **H** together in the needle or two strands of **E**.

TINY FLOWERS

Scatter small French knot flowers across the grasses, using two strands of **A**, alternating with two strands of **B** on the left-hand side and using two strands of **C** behind the achillea on the right-hand side.

FOREGROUND GRASSES

Work grasses across the foreground with straight stitch, using one strand of **J** then one or two strands of **M**, working the stitches at an angle and overlapping some of the alliums and achilleas.

FINISHING

Place the paper mount over the embroidery and check to ensure that the design is completed to your satisfaction. Work any additional stitches that may be needed.

Silver Birches

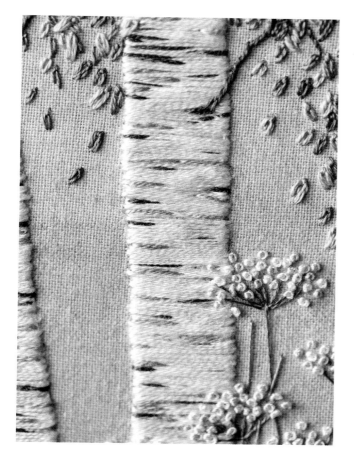

Graceful trunks of ghostly white rise through a
woodland garden of ferns and cow parsley.

The birch, most shy and lady-like of trees,
Her poverty, as best she may, retrieves,
And hints at her foregone gentilities
With some saved relics of her wealth of leaves

James Russell Lowell

This design uses
Back stitch
Fly stitch
French knot
Straight stitch
Whipped back stitch

The finished design
measures 20cm x 10cm
wide (8" x 4").

Requirements

30cm x 20cm wide (12" x 8") sheet of white paper

Paper scissors

Pins

Tracing paper

Fine black pen

HB pencil

Needles

No. 20 chenille

No. 5 crewel

No. 8 crewel

Threads

DMC stranded cotton

A = blanc

B = 10 vy lt tender green

C = 12 tender green

D = 648 lt beaver grey

E = 772 vy lt yellow-green

F = 935 vy dk avocado green

G = 3052 med green-grey

H = 3347 med yellow-green

I = 3348 lt yellow-green

J = 3362 dk pine green

K = 3363 med pine green

L = 3787 dk Jacobean green

DMC no. 8 perlé cotton

M = 3347 med yellow-green

Fabric

35cm x 25cm wide (14" x 10") piece of medium-weight calico (muslin)

Supplies

Slate frame or stretcher bars to fit fabric

Lacing thread (slate frame)

Thumbtacks (stretcher bars)

25cm x 15cm wide (10" x 6") piece of tear-away fabric stabiliser

Cerulean blue watercolour

Cadmium yellow watercolour

Palette or white plate

Large watercolour brush

Small watercolour brush

Ruler

Preparation for Embroidery

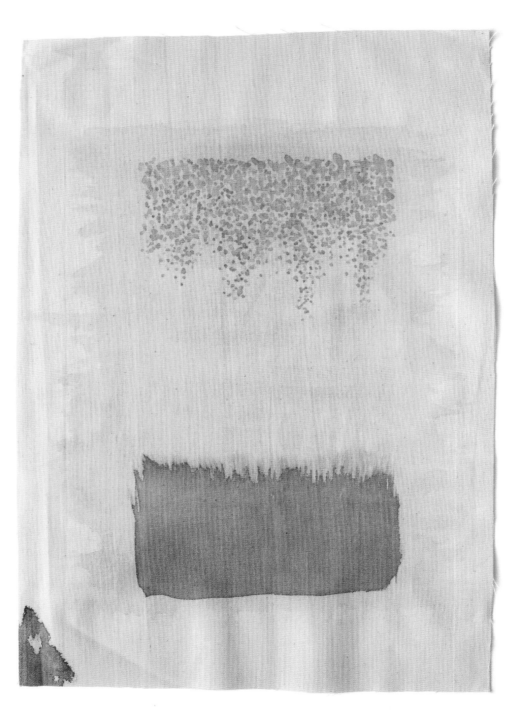

Preparing the fabric

Using the ruler and pencil, lightly mark the corners of a 25cm x 15cm wide (10" x 6") rectangle at the centre of the calico. Mix a small amount of cerulean blue watercolour with water on the palette and apply a blue wash to the marked rectangle. Allow to dry.

Mix a small amount of cadmium yellow with the remaining blue paint to create green. Add more water if necessary to create a green wash. Apply the wash to the lower third of the rectangle. Using the small brush paint wispy, irregular blades of grass into the sky.

Mix a second shade of green and paint a dappled leaf effect in the upper area using the two shades of green (fig 1).

Allow to dry on a flat surface. Press with an iron and pressing cloth.

At the centre of the sheet of paper, measure and mark a 20cm x 10cm wide (8" x 4") rectangle. Carefully cut away the paper from inside the rectangle. Position the paper mount over the painted fabric, moving it to frame the most pleasing section. Take care to ensure that the grainlines remain parallel with the cut edges of the paper. Mark each corner with a pin and remove the paper. Using the ruler and pencil, measure out 5mm (³⁄₁₆") from the marked point on each side and mark in a rectangle. It should measure 21cm x 11cm wide (8¼" x 4¼").

Transferring the design

Using the pencil, trace the trunk shaping and markings onto the tear away stabiliser.

Cut out the trunks, leaving them connected above the upper outline (diag 1).

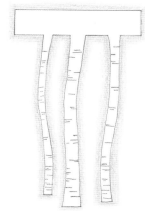

Position the trunks and hold in place with small stitches (fig 2).

Using the fine black pen, transfer the design to the tracing paper. Tape the tracing to a lightbox or window. Position the fabric over the tracing, ensuring that the design is centred within the marked rectangle and the trunks are aligned. Lightly transfer the branches and fern stems using the HB pencil. Mount the fabric into the frame ensuring it is drum tight.

Embroidery

Refer to the close-up photograph for colour and stitch placement.

Use the no. 20 chenille needle for the perlé cotton, the no. 5 crewel needle for three or four strands of thread and the no. 8 crewel for one or two strands of thread.

All embroidery is worked in the frame.

Order of work

> *Hint:* As you work, position the paper mount over the embroidery and pin in place. Prop your work up and leave it for 15-20 minutes. When you return, look at your stitching and you will be able to see any areas that need additional work.

SILVER BIRCH

Trunk

Using two strands of **A**, work back stitch along the edge of the stabiliser on both sides of the trunk. Using the same thread, cover the trunk with horizontal straight stitches, working over the back stitch outline. Stitch the fissures in the bark with straight stitches of varying lengths using two strands of **D** and **L** and the photographs as a guide to placement. Embroider the branches with whipped back stitch, using two strands of **L** for the large branches and one strand for the smaller ones. Work the remaining trunks in the same manner.

Leaves

Embroider the leaves with fly stitch, working the arms close together and using two strands of **H** then two strands of **I**. Add smaller leaves towards the tips of the branches using one strand of **H**

and **I**. Work additional leaves across the upper half of the leaf area with two strands of **J**.

GRASSES

Fill the foreground with vertical straight stitches using **F**, varying the length of the stitches by 1cm (⅜") and making the stitches approximately 2cm long (¾") at the sides, increasing to approximately 4cm (1½") and overlapping the central trunk.

- -

Note: Work the stitches in the same manner as laid work, making the first long stitch from the base upwards then taking a small stitch across to the tip of the next blade of grass and working it towards the base (diag 2).

This reduces bulk on the back of the work and uses much less thread.

Repeat with two strands of **J**. Working from the existing stitches and on each side of the central trunk, stitch a shorter row of straight stitches of varying lengths using one strand of **I**, taking care to ensure that the stitches are no longer than 1cm (⅜") and create a hazy line. Add another layer above the stitches just worked using one strand of **E**, merging them into the previous row. Work a dark area beneath the remaining two trunks with vertical straight stitches of varying lengths using one strand of **F** then one strand of **J** and finishing with one strand of **G**.

Embroider the grasses on the horizon, varying the length of the straight

stitches from 3cm-4cm (1⅛"-1½") and tucking the lower end of each stitch behind the existing stitches. Work a layer using one strand of **B** then a layer using one strand of **C** and finish with a layer using one strand of **G**.

FERNS

Work a line of back stitch along the centre of each fern frond using **L**. Beginning at the tip of the frond with a French knot and using one strand of **M**, work spaced straight stitches across the centre vein, increasing in length until approximately three quarters of the way down the frond then decreasing in length slightly to the base (diag 3).

Using the initial line of back stitch as a guide and one strand of **L**, bring the thread to the front just below the lower straight stitch. Slide the needle under the stitch and work a back stitch, pulling the straight stitch into a slight V.

Bring the thread to the front just below the next straight stitch. Slide the needle under the stitch and work a back stitch, pulling the straight stitch into a slight V and taking the thread to the back through the top of the first back stitch. Continue in this manner along the vein (diag 4).

Hint: Practise working a fern frond on a scrap of fabric to ensure that you have the spacing correct.

COW PARSLEY

Stitch the plants around the centre trunk, working the stems and umbels with fly stitch and straight stitch using one strand of **K** (diag 5).

Fill the umbels with French knots using two strands of **A**, adding knots worked with two strands of **B**.

Work the smaller plants in the background using one strand of **G** for the stems and umbels and one strand of **A** and **B** for the French knot flowers.

FOREGROUND GRASSES

Add grasses to the foreground with straight stitches working varying lengths and angles and using two strands of **B**, **C** and **I**. Finish with grasses worked with one strand of **C**.

FINISHING

Place the paper mount over the embroidery and check to ensure that the design is completed to your satisfaction. Work any additional stitches that may be needed.

Foxgloves

In every shade of pink, proud foxgloves stand sentinel over their garden companions.

"In no time the perennial borders were thick with rosy-pink foxglove and cream-coloured lilies, each of which hung on a pendant, collecting dew on its satiny petals."

Alice Hoffman

This Design Uses
Detached chain
Finger chain
French knot
Ribbon stitch
Spider web rose
Straight stitch

The finished design measures 10cm x 20cm wide (4" x 8").

Requirements

Fabric

25cm x 35cm wide (10" x 14") piece of medium-weight calico (muslin)

Supplies

Slate frame or stretcher bars to fit fabric

Lacing thread (slate frame)

Thumb tacks (stretcher bars)

Alizarin crimson watercolour

Ultramarine blue watercolour

Cadmium yellow watercolour

Palette or white plate

Large watercolour brush

Small watercolour brush

Ruler

20cm x 30cm wide (8" x 12") sheet of white paper

Paper scissors

Pins

Tracing paper

Fine black pen

HB pencil

Needles

No. 18 chenille

No. 20 chenille

No. 24 chenille

No. 5 crewel

No. 8 crewel

Threads & Ribbons

DMC stranded cotton

A = blanc

B = 14 pale apple green

C = 23 apple blossom

D = 209 lavender

E = 211 lt lavender

F = 333 vy dk blue-violet

G = 341 lt blue-violet

H = 368 lt pistachio green

I = 520 dk fern green

J = 524 vy lt fern green

K = 935 vy dk avocado green

L = 3348 lt yellow-green

M = 3363 med pine green

N = 3688 med tea rose

O = 3727 lt antique mauve

P = 3807 cornflower blue

Di van Niekerk 2mm silk ribbon

Q = 33 autumn

R = 45 dusty pink

S = 88 royal blue

T = 103 white

U = 124 protea grey

Di van Niekerk 4mm silk ribbon

V = 45 dusty pink

W = 126 forest shade

Di van Niekerk 7mm silk ribbon

X = 42 peony

Y = 44 rose ash

Z = 122 touch of pink

Preparation for Embroidery

Preparing the fabric

Using the ruler and pencil, lightly mark the corners of a 15cm x 25cm wide (6" x 10") rectangle at the centre of the calico. Mix a small amount of ultramarine blue watercolour with water on the palette and apply a blue wash to the marked rectangle. Allow to dry slightly.

Mix a small amount of alizarin crimson with water and apply in places allowing it to seep into the blue to create a softly shaded sky. Allow to dry on a flat surface. Mix a small amount of cadmium yellow with the remaining blue paint to create green. Add more water if necessary to create a green wash. Apply the wash to approximately the lower half of the rectangle.

Using the small brush paint wispy, irregular blades of grass into the sky, making them slightly higher at the ends (fig 1).

Allow to dry on a flat surface. Press with an iron and pressing cloth.

At the centre of the sheet of paper, measure and mark a 10cm x 20cm wide (4" x 8") rectangle. Carefully cut away the paper from inside the rectangle. Position the paper mount over the painted fabric, moving it to frame the most pleasing section. Take care to ensure that the grainlines remain parallel with the cut edges of the paper. Mark each corner with a pin and remove the paper. Using the ruler and pencil, measure out 5mm (³⁄₁₆") from the marked point on each side and mark in a rectangle. It should measure 11cm x 21cm wide (4⅛" x 8¼"). This is the area that will be embroidered.

Transferring the design

Using the fine black pen, transfer the design onto tracing paper. Tape the tracing to a lightbox or window. Centre the rectangle on the fabric over the tracing and tape in place. Lightly transfer the design using the HB pencil. Mount the fabric into the frame ensuring that it is drum tight.

Embroidery

Refer to the close-up photograph for colour and stitch placement.

Use the no. 18 chenille needle for the 7mm ribbon, the no. 20 chenille for the 4mm ribbon, the no. 24 chenille for the 2mm ribbon, the no. 5 crewel needle for three strands of thread and the no. 8 crewel for one or two strands of thread.

All embroidery is worked in the frame.

Order of work

Hint: As you work, position the paper mount over the embroidery and pin in place. Prop your work up and leave it for 15-20 minutes. When you return, look at your stitching and you will be able to see any areas that need additional work.

BACKGROUND GRASSES

Beginning at the base line and using three strands of **K**, cover the lower half of the green area with vertical straight stitches, varying the length of each stitch slightly and making the stitches 5cm-6cm (2"-2⅜") towards the ends of the rectangle, curving down to 4cm-5cm (1½"-2") at the centre.

- -

NOTE: Work the stitches in the same manner as laid work, making the first long stitch from the base upwards then taking a small stitch across to the tip of the next blade of grass and working it towards the base (diag 1).

This reduces bulk on the back of the work and uses much less thread.

Repeat this process using three strands of **M**, crossing the previous stitches and filling any gaps.

Using two strands of **I**, work another layer of spaced straight stitches, extending them 2cm (¾") past the first layers at the upper edge and tucking the lower ends behind the existing stitches. Repeat this process using two strands of **M**, crossing the previous layer. The grasses should now be approximately 7cm-8cm tall (2¾"-3⅛") at each side of the rectangle.

Using the photograph as a guide and one strand of **H** and **M**, work longer straight stitches across the horizon, making the stitches reach approximately 2cm-3cm (¾"-1⅛") above the main background stitches and tucking the ends behind the existing stitches.

FOXGLOVES

Each flower is worked with a variation of a detached chain with the loop worked with ribbon and the anchoring stitch with one strand of a coordinating cotton thread. Make each anchoring stitch a little longer than normal so that the ribbon has room to spread.

Take care not to pull the ribbon loop too tight. It should sit up on the fabric and be quite rounded. Work one or two small straight stitches at the top of each flower and the green buds with French knots or small straight stitches using the foliage colour. The pink buds are stitched with French knots or small straight stitches and the leaves are worked with ribbon stitch, beginning with smaller leaves approximately halfway down the stem. Work larger leaves at the base.

Use the following information as a guide to ribbon and thread colours for each element.

LEFT-HAND SPIRES x 3: flowers and buds – **O**, **R** and **V**, foliage – **Q**

LEFT-HAND SPIRE x 1: flowers – **Z**, foliage – **W**

RIGHT-HAND FOREGROUND x 3: flowers – **X**, foliage – **W**

RIGHT-HAND BACKGROUND x 2: flowers – **Y**, foliage – **W**

ROSES

Work each open flower with a spider web rose, using **O** to work five spokes and **R** to weave the rose. Stitch each bud with a French knot using the same ribbon, varying the tension to create buds of different sizes. Embroider the foliage with ribbon stitch using **Q**.

LAVENDER

Stitch the flowers with irregular columns of French knots using one strand of **D** and **F** together in the needle or one strand of **G** and **P** together in the needle.

LAMB'S EAR

Stitch the flowers with irregular columns of French knots using one strand of **D** and **E** together in the needle. Work the stalks with straight stitch using two strands of **J** and the leaves with straight stitch using **U**.

HAREBELLS

Purple harebells

Embroider the larger flowers with **S**, working 4-5 small ribbon stitches and work the stems with straight stitch using two strands of **H**. Stitch the green and purple buds with French knots using the same threads. Work the smaller, background flowers with straight stitch using one strand of **D** and **P** together in the needle. Stitch the buds with French knots using the same threads.

White harebells

Work the large flowers in the same manner as the purple harebells, using **T** for the ribbon stitches and French knot buds and two strands of **M** for the stems. Stitch the smaller, background flowers with straight stitch and French knots using two strands of **C**.

SEEDED GRASS

Work each seed head with a finger chain using one strand of **B** and **L** and following the step-by-step instructions on page 132. Once the chain is secured, anchor the thread with a long stitch to form the stem. Add straight stitch grass using the same threads.

SMALL FLOWERS

Scatter French knot flowers behind the foreground foxglove on the left-hand side using two strands of **A** and **C**, working some two-wrap knots.

Stitch French knots beneath the roses using two strands of **B** or **L**. Add French knots above the lavender using one strand of **C** and **O** together in the needle.

On the right-hand side embroider French knots behind the foxglove using one strand of **C** and **N** together in the needle.

FINISHING

Place the paper mount over the embroidery and check to ensure that the design is completed to your satisfaction. Work any additional stitches that may be needed.

Cow Parsley

The delicate lace of white cow parsley flowers decorates a field of wheat.

"If you truly love nature, you will find beauty everywhere."

Vincent van Gogh

This Design Uses
Detached chain
French knot
Whipped back stitch

The finished design measures 20cm x 10cm wide (8" x 4").

Requirements

Fabric

35cm x 25cm wide (14" x 10") piece of medium-weight calico (muslin)

Supplies

Slate frame or stretcher bars to fit fabric

Lacing thread (slate frame)

Thumb tacks (stretcher bars)

Ultramarine blue watercolour

Cadmium yellow watercolour

Palette or white plate

Large watercolour brush

Small watercolour brush

Ruler

30cm x 20cm wide (12" x 8") sheet of white paper

Paper scissors

Pins

Tracing paper

Fine black pen

HB pencil

Needle

No. 8 crewel

Threads

DMC stranded cotton

 A = blanc

 B = 10 vy lt tender green

 C = 11 lt tender green

 D = 3348 lt yellow-green

 E = 3362 dk pine green

 F = 3364 pine green

Preparation for Embroidery

Preparing the fabric

Using the ruler and pencil, lightly mark the corners of a 25cm x 15cm wide (10" x 6") rectangle at the centre of the calico. Mix a small amount of cadmium yellow watercolour with water on the palette and apply a yellow wash to the marked rectangle. Allow to dry slightly.

Mix a small amount of ultramarine blue with the remaining yellow paint to create green. Add more water if necessary to create a green wash. Apply the green with the edge of the large brush, dabbing it onto the lower area of the rectangle and extending up the left-hand side. The green should blend into the yellow as the fabric is still damp. Allow to dry a little more. Mix several shades of green on the palette and, using the small brush, paint wispy, irregular blades of grass of different lengths, angling them towards the right-hand side. You may need to allow the fabric to dry a little between each to prevent excessive colour bleeding.

Allow to dry on a flat surface. Using the remaining green on the palette, load the small brush with colour and flick the bristles to splatter the fabric with paint. Repeat with several shades of green (fig 1).

Allow to dry on a flat surface and press with an iron and pressing cloth.

At the centre of the sheet of paper, measure and mark a 20cm x 10cm wide (8" x 4") rectangle. Carefully cut away the paper from inside the rectangle. Position the paper mount over the painted fabric, moving it to frame the most pleasing section. Take care to ensure that the grainlines remain parallel with the cut edges of the paper. Mark each corner with a pin and remove the paper. Using the ruler and pencil, measure out 5mm (3⁄16") from the marked point on each side and mark in a rectangle. It should measure 21cm x 11cm wide (8 ¼" x 4 ¼"). This is the area that will be embroidered.

Transferring the design

Using the fine black pen, transfer the design to the tracing paper. Tape the tracing to a lightbox or window. Position the fabric over the tracing, ensuring that the design is centred within the marked rectangle. Lightly transfer the design using the HB pencil.

Mount the fabric into the frame ensuring it is drum tight.

Embroidery

Refer to the close-up photograph for colour and stitch placement.

All embroidery is worked in the frame.

Order of work

Hint: As you work, position the paper mount over the embroidery and pin in place. Prop your work up and leave it for 15-20 minutes. When you return, look at your stitching and you will be able to see any areas that need additional work.

COW PARSLEY

Stems and umbels

Stitch the stems and umbels with whipped back stitch using one strand of **E**.

Flowers

Work the flowers with two-wrap French knots using two strands of **A**. Stitch extra two-wrap French knots using two strands of **B**.

WHEAT

Stitch the wheat ears with detached chain, offsetting the stitches to one another and using one strand of **C**, **D**, **E** and **F**. Work the stems with whipped back stitch using the same threads.

FINISHING

Place the paper mount over the embroidery and check to ensure that the design is completed to your satisfaction. Work any additional stitches that may be needed.

Poppies & Cornflowers

Papery, pink skirts of poppy flowers twirl amongst the cornflowers.

Through the dancing poppies stole A breeze, most softly lulling to my soul.

John Keats

This Design Uses
Detached blanket stitch
French knot
Pistil stitch
Straight stitch

The finished design measures
14cm (5 ½") square.

Pink Poppies and Cornflowers

Cornflowers

Requirements

Fabric

30cm (12") square of medium-weight calico (muslin)

Supplies

Slate frame, stretcher bars to fit fabric or a 25cm (10") embroidery hoop

Lacing thread (slate frame)

Thumbtacks (stretcher bars)

Cobalt blue watercolour

Cadmium yellow watercolour

Palette or white plate

Large watercolour brush

Small watercolour brush

Ruler

20cm (8") square of white paper

Paper scissors

Pins

HB pencil

Needles

No. 5 crewel

No. 8 crewel

Threads

DMC stranded cotton

A = 335 rose

B = 368 lt pistachio green

C = 761 lt salmon

D = 772 vy lt yellow-green

E = 792 dk cornflower blue

F = 794 lt cornflower blue

G = 818 baby pink

H = 935 vy dk avocado green

I = 3053 green-grey

J = 3350 ultra dk dusky rose

K = 3362 dk pine green

L = 3363 med pine green

M = 3807 cornflower blue

N = 3833 lt strawberry

O = 3840 lt China blue

Preparation for Embroidery

Preparing the fabric

Using the ruler and pencil, lightly mark the corners of a 20cm (8") square at the centre of the calico. Mix a small amount of cobalt blue watercolour with water on the palette and apply a blue wash to the marked square. Allow to dry.

Mix a small amount of cadmium yellow with the remaining blue paint to create green. Add more water if necessary to create a green wash. Apply the wash to approximately the lower third of the square. Using the small brush paint wispy, irregular blades of grass into the sky, making them slightly higher at the ends (fig 1).

Allow to dry on a flat surface.

Press with an iron and pressing cloth.

At the centre of the sheet of paper, measure and mark a 14cm (5½") square. Carefully cut away the paper from inside the square. Position the paper mount over the painted fabric, moving it to frame the most pleasing section. Take care to ensure that the grainlines remain parallel with the cut edges of the paper. Mark each corner with a pin and remove the paper. Using the ruler and pencil, measure out 5mm (³⁄₁₆") from the marked point on each side and mark in a square. It should measure 15cm (6") square. This is the area that will be embroidered.

Mount the fabric into the frame or hoop ensuring that it is drum tight.

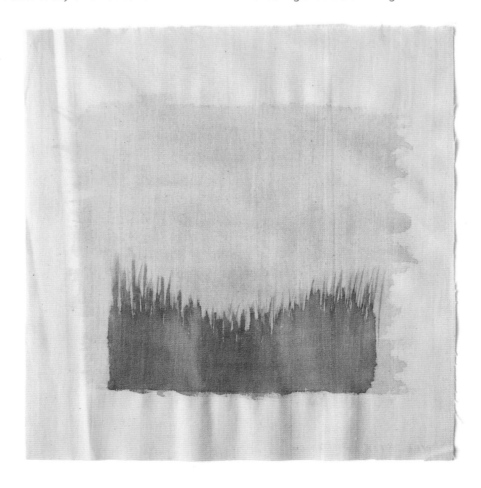

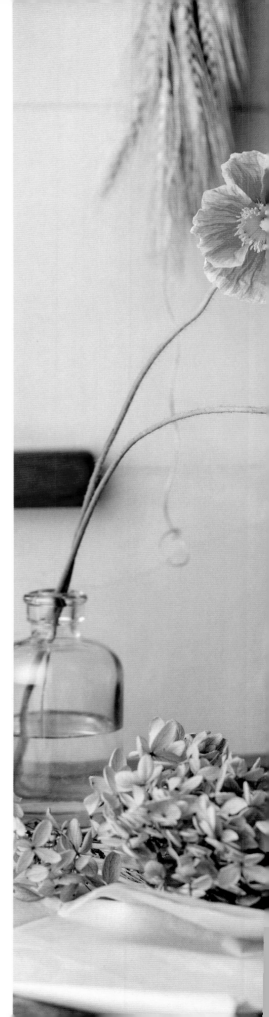

129

Embroidery

Refer to the close-up photograph for colour and stitch placement.

Use the no. 5 crewel needle for three strands of thread and the no. 8 crewel for one or two strands of thread.

All embroidery is worked in a frame or hoop.

Order of work

> *Hint*: As you work, position the paper mount over the embroidery and pin in place. Prop your work up and leave it for 15-20 minutes. When you return, look at your stitching and you will be able to see any areas that need additional work.

BACKGROUND GRASSES

Using three strands of **H**, work long, vertical straight stitches, varying the length by approximately 1cm (⅜"), across the lower third of the square, echoing the green colour wash.

- - - - - - - - - - - - - - - - - - - -

NOTE: Work the stitches in the same manner as laid work, making the first long stitch from the base upwards then taking a small stitch across to the tip of the next blade of grass and working it towards the base (diag 1).

This reduces bulk on the back of the work and uses much less thread.

Repeat with three strands of **K**, filling any gaps. Using two strands of **L**, add more length to the grasses, working up to 5cm (2") beyond the skyline on each side and 2cm (¾") at the centre. Add finer grasses along the horizon using one strand of **B**, **D** and **K**, following the curve.

CORNFLOWERS

Work each cornflower with straight stitches radiating from the centre and using three strands of thread, combining the listed colours in the needle or using three strands of **M**. Use the paler blues and smaller stitches in the background changing to darker blues and longer stitches in the foreground. Work the cornflowers using the following combinations of threads:

Two strands	One strand
E	F
F	M
F	O
M	F
O	M

Add straight stitch stems with one or two strands of **I** and **L**.

POPPIES

Work each poppy with straight stitches radiating from the centre, combining the listed colours in the needle. Use two strands of thread and 6-8 stitches for the smaller background flowers, three strands and 8-10 stitches for the medium flowers and three strands and 10-14 stitches for the large flowers.

Two strands	One strand
N	A
G	C
N	C
C	G
A	J
A	N
C	N

Embroider the poppy stems with pistil stitch using two strands of **I** and **L**, tucking the base of the stem behind the existing stitches.

WHEAT

The wheat ears are worked with detached blanket stitch using two strands of **D** and **I**. Work the straight stitch foundation approximately 1cm (⅜") long and cover with detached blanket stitch. Stitch each stalk with a long straight stitch using one strand of the same colour.

GRASSES

Work additional grasses using one strand of **B**, **D** and **I**, varying the lengths and angles. Scatter French knots amongst the grasses using two strands of **D** and **I**.

FINISHING

Place the paper mount over the embroidery and check to ensure that the design is completed to your satisfaction. Work any additional stitches that may be needed.

Stitch Index

FINGER CHAIN

This technique creates a very fine, neat chain that is perfect for seeded grasses.

1 / Emerge at A. Leaving a loop, take the thread to the back through the same hole. Emerge close to A and remove the needle.

2 / While holding the thread, reach through the loop with thumb and forefinger of the other hand and begin to pull the thread through, tightening the first loop. Do not release the new loop or thread.

3 / Maintaining tension on the thread, pull the new loop to close the first into a small chain against the fabric. Do not release the loop or thread.

4 / Reach through the loop, and begin to pull the thread through, dropping the previous loop. Do not release the new loop or thread.

5 / Maintaining tension on the thread, pull the new loop to close the previous one into a small chain against the first chain. Do not release the loop or thread.

6 / Repeat steps 4-5 until the chain is the desired length.

7 / To finish the chain, pull the thread completely through the last loop and tighten.

8 / Take the thread to the back the desired distance away to form a stem.

DETACHED BLANKET STITCH

These seed heads are embroidered across the meadow and add wonderful texture.

1 / Work a foundation with a straight stitch from A to B. Emerge just to the left of A.

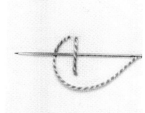

2 / Loop the thread to the left and take the needle from right to left behind the straight stitch. Do not pierce the fabric. The thread is under the needle tip.

3 / Pull the thread through until the stitch wraps snugly around the foundation

4 / Work the next stitch in the same manner, ensuring the stitch lies beside the first stitch but does not overlap it.

5 / Continue working in the same manner until the foundation is covered.

6 / Take the thread to the back to form the stalk.

RIBBON STITCH

Ribbon stitch creates beautiful petals or leaves with curled tips. The appearance of the stitch depends on the placement of the needle through the ribbon and the tension of the ribbon. For stitches with more height, work the stitches with a loose tension or over a laying tool.

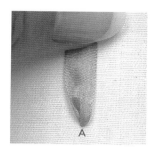

1 / Bring the ribbon to the front at A. Hold the ribbon on the fabric with your thumb.

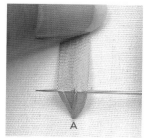

2 / Place the needle under the ribbon near A. Using a slight upward pressure, move the needle towards your thumb to smooth and spread the ribbon.

3 / Place the tip of the needle in the centre of the ribbon at the position for the tip of the stitch (B).

4 / Take the needle to the back. Place your thumb over the stitch to keep it untwisted. Begin to gently pull the ribbon through.

continued next page...

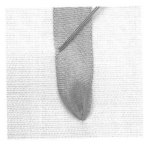
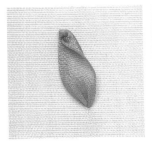

5 / Pull until the ribbon folds back on itself at the tip and the edges curl.

6 / Side ribbon stitch. Place the tip of the needle just in from the edge of the ribbon at the position for the tip of the stitch.

7 / Take the needle to the back and pull the ribbon through as for steps 4 and 5.

8 / By placing the needle on the other side of the ribbon the tip of the stitch will curl in the opposite direction.

SPIDER WEB ROSE

This easy to stitch, textured rose is created by weaving the ribbon through a framework of five straight stitches.

1 / Petals. Tie a knot in the end of the ribbon. Bring it to the front between two spokes close to the centre.

2 / Working in a counter clockwise direction, weave the ribbon over and under the spokes of the framework until one round is complete.

3 / Pull the ribbon firmly so the framework does not show at the centre.

4 / Work 1 to 2 more rounds in the same manner, maintaining the over and under sequence.

5 / Using looser tension and allowing the ribbon to twist, work until the framework is hidden. Take the needle to the back.

6 / Pull the ribbon through and secure on the back of the work.

WHIPPED CHAIN STITCH

Work a line of chain or reverse chain stitch. Use a tapestry needle for the whipping.

1 / Emerge at the end of the line and slide the needle down beneath the first chain.

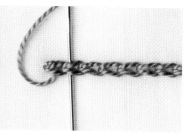

2 / Pull the thread through. Slide the needle down beneath the next chain.

3 / Repeat along the line and take the thread to the back and secure.

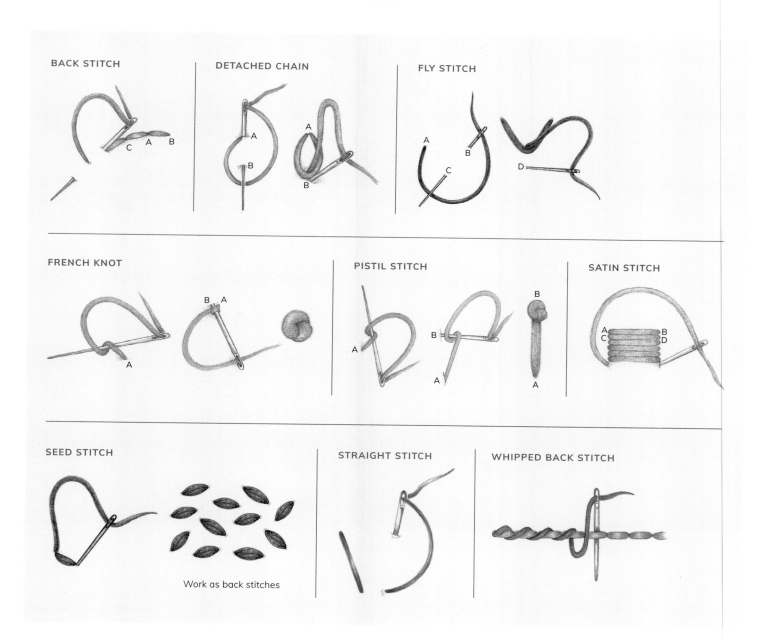

BACK STITCH

DETACHED CHAIN

FLY STITCH

FRENCH KNOT

PISTIL STITCH

SATIN STITCH

SEED STITCH

Work as back stitches

STRAIGHT STITCH

WHIPPED BACK STITCH

Kits

SEASCAPE

Page 12
Kit contains: Fabric panels, embroidery threads, ribbons and needles

HOLLYHOCKS

Page 22
Kit contains: Fabric panels, embroidery threads and needle

BLUEBELLS UNDER THE BIRCHES

Page 32
Kit contains: Fabric panels, embroidery threads, ribbons and needles

TOPIARY IN THE BORDER

Page 42
Kit contains: Fabric panels, fabric stabiliser, embroidery threads, ribbons and needles

AMONGST THE DAISIES

Page 52
Kit contains: Fabric panels, embroidery threads and needles

IRISES

Page 62
Kit contains: Fabric panels, embroidery threads, ribbons and needles

COTTAGE GARDEN

Page 72
Kit contains: Fabric panels, embroidery threads and needles

ALLIUMS & TOPIARY

Page 84
Kit contains: Fabric panels, fabric stabiliser, embroidery threads and needles

SILVER BIRCHES

Page 94
Kit contains: Fabric panels, fabric stabiliser, embroidery threads and needles

FOXGLOVES

Page 104
Kit contains: Fabric panels, embroidery threads, ribbons and needles

COW PARSLEY

Page 114
Kit contains: Fabric panels, embroidery threads and needle

POPPIES & CORNFLOWERS

Page 122
Kit contains: Fabric panels, embroidery threads and needles

About me

In 1999, when I was eight months pregnant, I spotted the embroidery magazine Inspirations (issue 23) with a cover featuring a hand-embroidered herbaceous garden. It reminded me of the tablecloths and linens of my grandmother's generation that I loved. Despite anticipating little opportunity to produce needlework once my baby was born, I bought the magazine and stored it away thinking that one day I would make something along those lines. Sadly, one year later I had all the time in the world. Our daughter Emily was diagnosed with a genetic condition and died at ten months old.

It was obviously a very traumatic time. I had empty arms and needed a therapy. As a distraction I turned to the embroidery magazine. The need to keep both head and hands busy was met perfectly with embroidery and I discovered the way I could express myself creatively using a traditional craft.

I have always loved to sew. Creating clothes was my first sewing love when I was a teenager. Encouraged by my enthusiastic sewing teacher at school, who now can't believe my stitches are so small and neat, I then went on to study fashion at college, followed by ten years working as a Ladies wear Designer/Pattern cutter based in London.

So, from the magazine and remembering the basic embroidery stitches taught to me at school, I began to create my own style, stitching intricate flowers from foxgloves and daisies to meadow grasses and cow parsley onto linens and my hand-painted cotton backgrounds.

Taking inspiration from the countryside and gardens, I fill my scrapbooks with sketches and pictures for reference and colour combinations. I paint the background fabric, select my thread colours and start building the background layers, introducing the flowers and details in the foreground, adding subtle effects such as combining two threads of different colours in the same needle. It can take days and weeks to complete a picture but I have found a creative outlet that I truly love.

ACKNOWLEDGEMENTS

A huge thank you to Inspirations Studios for inspiring me
over the years and asking me to inspire others.
Thank you for your support.

Thank you to my parents; they gave me a love of flowers
but it's a shame I missed out on the gardening gene!

Thank you to Tricia (Mrs B!) my favourite school teacher.
She enthusiastically taught me many sewing skills and
is now a family friend.

And lastly to my very patient husband Nick,
and our gorgeous daughter Sophie
Thank you for your love, support and patience.

In memory of Emily.